Sex Beyond "Yes"

ALSO BY QUILL R KUKLA

City Living: How Urban Spaces and Urban Dwellers Make One Another

'Yo!' and 'Lo!': The Pragmatic Topography of the Space of Reasons

Mass Hysteria: Medicine, Culture and Mothers' Bodies

NORTON
SHORTS

Sex Beyond "Yes"

Pleasure and Agency for Everyone

QUILL R KUKLA

W. W. NORTON & COMPANY
Independent Publishers Since 1923

Copyright © 2025 by Quill R Kukla

All rights reserved
Printed in the United States of America
First Edition

For information about permission to reproduce selections from
this book, write to Permissions, W. W. Norton & Company, Inc.,
500 Fifth Avenue, New York, NY 10110

For information about special discounts for bulk purchases, please
contact W. W. Norton Special Sales at specialsales@wwnorton.com or
800-233-4830

Manufacturing by Lakeside Book Company
Production manager: Delaney Adams

ISBN: 978-1-324-06492-3

W. W. Norton & Company, Inc.
500 Fifth Avenue, New York, NY 10110
www.wwnorton.com

W. W. Norton & Company Ltd.
15 Carlisle Street, London W1D 3BS

10 9 8 7 6 5 4 3 2 1

For Dan Steinberg, who never bores me.

CONTENTS

CHAPTER 1: Beyond Consent   1

CHAPTER 2: Sex Talk   21

CHAPTER 3: Scaffolding Good Sex   37

CHAPTER 4: Imperfect Autonomy   53

CHAPTER 5: Ambivalence and Agency   72

CHAPTER 6: Extractive Sex and Rape Culture   86

CHAPTER 7: Sex Work and Sexual Contracts   100

CHAPTER 8: Domination, Submission, and Power Play   115

ACKNOWLEDGMENTS   135

NOTES   137

READINGS IN CONVERSATION   145

FOR FURTHER EXPLORATION   151

INDEX   155

Sex Beyond "Yes"

CHAPTER 1

Beyond Consent

✖   ✖   ✖   ✖   ✖   ✖   ✖

A young woman who thinks of herself as a feminist fantasizes about her new boyfriend tying her up. The idea of being helpless and at his mercy makes her feel sexy. One day, as they are messing around, he takes out ropes and slowly begins to tie her with them. She is pretty sure he would stop if she asked him to or struggled, but she doesn't. He proceeds. She finds the whole thing a huge turn-on, but also worries that her desire for submission and his desire for domination might both be sexist. She wonders why she wants this kind of play, and why he does.

An eighty-seven-year-old man with moderate dementia often forgets that he lives in a long-term care facility. Sometimes he recognizes his husband, who comes to visit, and sometimes he does not. But when he has sex with his husband, he responds with obvious pleasure and affection, and he often asks for his husband when he is alone. Today his husband asks him if he is feeling sexy, and he says "yes," and they make love.

After a lifetime of feeling unattractive and an evening of moderate drinking, a middle-aged man who has always been a bit of a loner is approached by a younger woman in a bar. She asks him if he wants to fuck her in the alley. He feels awkward and not really turned on, but he worries that turning her down would be ungrateful and unmanly. He also wonders if he will ever get another chance for this kind of an encounter, so he goes with her.

Are these stories of good sex? Ethical sex? Consensual sex? Do the people in these stories have *sexual agency*—that is, are their actions in these situations self-determining, self-expressive, and not hijacked by anyone else's goals or desires or by manipulative social pressures? I expect that each of the stories will make readers uneasy; they are not ethically clean, and they might end up involving harm. At the same time, each of them has the potential to turn out to be a story about sexual joy and fulfillment. What more would we want to know about these people, their communication with one another, and their situations to decide if these are stories about sex going well or poorly? How could each of the stories above turn out to affirm or undercut sexual agency, depending on the details?

So many of our conversations about sexual ethics and sexual agency focus on *consent*. But notice that in these scenarios, whether everyone consented is not really what we need to know. It is already clear that in the first scenario there was no moment of explicit verbal consent but also that the woman does not try to stop her boyfriend from proceeding or show any distress. In the second scenario, knowing that the man with dementia said the word *yes* does not help much with our unease, which is about sense of self, competence, and vulnerability. In the third scenario, the man certainly seems to be acting under his own free will, but our discomfort remains. It is always necessary that everyone in a sexual encounter is participating freely and voluntarily. And of course, if someone makes clear that they do not want to participate in a sexual activity, then it is never okay for it to proceed. But the narrow question, "Did they say 'yes' to sex?" is not the most pressing one we need answered before we can judge whether the complex sexual encounters in these scenarios went well.

Here are some different questions you might have about the people in the opening stories:

How long have the young woman and her boyfriend been together, and how good is he at reading and responding to any signs she might give that she is uncomfortable or wants to stop? Did he already know that she fantasized about bondage? Do they have a sexist dynamic outside of the bedroom? Can they talk to one another about their desires and how these might play into gender stereotypes? Could she easily and safely leave if she wanted to? Does she have a community with which she can talk about her feminist qualms with bondage and her attraction to it, or would she be slut-shamed or called out as a bad feminist for bringing the topic up?

As for the older man with dementia and his husband, how good is the visiting husband at understanding and respecting when his partner is aware of his surroundings and able to make decisions, and when he isn't? Does this long-term care facility support its residents' sexual desires and agency, or does the couple have to sneak sex on the sly? Is there a support team who can give medical advice about his state of mind and who will provide help if anything goes wrong?

And finally, when it comes to the man in the alley, does he find the encounter thrilling and affirming, or depressing? How drunk is he? Does the woman treat their encounter as a fun adventure, or does she ultimately humiliate him? He chooses to have sex even though he feels ambivalent, but does he also feel like he could choose otherwise?

4   SEX BEYOND "YES"

If she harmed him, would he be too embarrassed to get help? Does he treat her well?

Whether these are stories of good or bad sex, ethical or exploitative sex, free or unfree sex depends on all these details and more.

This is a book about good sex. I want to explore how we can expand and protect our own and one another's sexual agency and pleasure, and enjoy wanted, satisfying, ethically sound sex. Although some people are asexual (that is, they do not experience sexual attraction or desire), sex is a basic and important source of pleasure, fulfillment, and self-expression for most people. A society that supports human flourishing will make opportunities for people to access sexual pleasure and to exercise sexual agency in safe and ethical ways. At the same time, sex is an arena in which people are vulnerable and especially open to exploitation, injury, coercion, and other kinds of harm. Protecting ourselves against bad sex is central to enjoying good sex, and an ethics of promoting sexual pleasure and agency can never be fully separate from an ethics of avoiding sexual violation and harm. So, this book will discuss both good and bad sex, sex that goes right and sex that goes wrong. But, while I will not avoid or deny the reality and seriousness of bad sex, sexual assault, and rape, I want to focus first and foremost on sexual pleasure, sexual agency, and sex that goes well for everyone.

As a culture, we are obsessed with bad sex and how to protect against it, and we talk about that almost to the exclusion of talking about good sex and how to have it. Most sex education today and most academic literature on sexual ethics, including feminist writing about sexual consent, focus overwhelmingly on rape, sexual violation, and nonconsensual sex. Almost every recent popular or academic book on sexual consent and sexual agency begins with a litany of examples of bad sex, rape, misogynist violence, and consent gone wrong. This work

BEYOND CONSENT 5

is necessary, but it tends to assume that our main goal is to ward off any risk of bad or unethical sex, no matter the cost, and no matter how much sexual exploration, pleasure, and freedom we have to give up along the way. Any uncertainty or ambiguity or messiness around sex is taken as a reason not to have it. Slogans like "'Maybe' means no!" abound.

So much discussion around sex is focused on how to *refuse* it effectively, and on the importance of respecting people's refusals, one might easily get the impression that sexual agency is about the ability to effectively say "no" to sex, and in particular about women's ability to say "no" to men. But most of us, including most women, often want to have sex. Being able to have good sex enhances our agency. We need more discussion about how to make sex good and not just about how to avoid sexual harm. We try to teach teenagers and college students about the dangers of sex and the wrongs of rape, but we don't offer them tools for exploring sexual pleasure and possibilities, nor for building and strengthening their sexual agency. Having good sex and helping our partners have good sex are complicated skills; we are not born with them, but rather we must learn and practice them. We should be as well-versed in how to have good sex as we are in how sex can go awry.

Although I am an academic philosopher, over time, I have become increasingly impatient with the abstract, disengaged ways in which academics typically discuss bodies, freedom, consent, and pleasure. My goal here is to use my philosophical toolbox to write about sex in ways that are concrete and useful. For many years I have participated in alternative sex communities, in which queer, trans, and kinky folks thoughtfully and intentionally explore sexual activities that go beyond the so-called vanilla norm of monogamous heterosexual missionary sex in a domestic bedroom. I have attended alternative sex conventions, meet-ups, and seminars and have befriended sex educators and sex workers. I've been impressed with how explicitly reflective these communities are about their practices, and about the techniques they use to protect and promote sexual agency and exploration, while protecting people from harm. I want to share and build upon what I have learned about sex in these contexts.

Queer sex, experimental sex, casual hookup sex, group sex, and sex between people of any gender and with any body type are just as central to understanding the dynamics and ethics of sexual agency as is traditional monogamous heterosexual sex. Our established approach to talking about sex, which takes heterosexual sex as the paradigm and understands everything else as a variation, is out of date in any case. Less than 50 percent of Generation Z (people born between roughly 1997 and 2012) identifies as cisgender and heterosexual, according to recent American surveys. When sex education and discussions of sexual ethics focus solely on sex between cisgender men and women, or treat it as the norm, we are simply not speaking to the needs, questions, and experiences of young people. More generally, we all need tools for negotiating what we want to do with one another, discovering and protecting our own boundaries, exploring new experiences safely, and expanding our agency. While this book focuses overwhelmingly on sex, I hope it will be clear that much of what I have to say is broadly applicable to all the situations we face in which good communication and collaboration and strong agency and boundaries matter.

Much of the public discussion about sexual agency and ethics is framed around the importance of being able to say "yes" or "no" to sex and having this answer respected. Many of us grew up hearing "'No' means no!" as a slogan that was almost synonymous with protecting sexual agency. But this is such a low bar; just because we don't say "no" to sex does not mean that sex is what we want or that the sex is good. Over the last several years, sex educators and advocates fighting sexual violence have worked to replace the old "'No' means no" standard with the notion of *affirmative consent*, which is the idea that someone must actively and freely say "yes" to a sexual activity for it to be consensual. Often, people use the phrase "'Yes' means yes" to capture this notion. In the last decade, affirmative consent has become a legal standard in many places. This is an improvement over the old standard, as it makes clear that sexual agency involves doing things we choose to do, not just failing to resist. But both these slogans focus on letting people decide when to agree to sex, rather than on how to make it good.

So much of what we need to say to one another to make sex genuinely good, pleasureful, and respectful doesn't take the form of a yes-or-no question. Often it consists of questions such as What do you like? How do you enjoy being touched? Is there anywhere that you hate being touched? What are your limits and boundaries? When you are uncomfortable, how do you tend to act so that I can keep an eye out for that? We need to talk to one another in order to explore what we want to do and how to do it well together. Much of good sexual communication is not about asking questions or giving answers at all: We should be building fantasies together, flirting, expressing our concern and affection for one another, and establishing trust. The narrow focus on "yes" and "no" in sex education hides all this talking and its importance. Telling people to wait for a "yes" before proceeding tells us nothing about how to lay the groundwork for good sex.

By *consensual* sex, I mean sex where everyone involved is participating of their own free will and is communicating that to everyone else, whether verbally or through body language, and where everyone would stop if someone ceased to make it clear that they were participating

8   SEX BEYOND "YES"

freely. During consensual sex, we demonstrate to our partner that this is what we want to be doing, and our partner makes it clear that they will continue only for as long as we are still showing that we want to continue. Sex with agency and consensual sex are related and ideally symbiotic, but not the same. I could be participating in sex consensually but not really in a way that expresses my agency. For example, I may legitimately choose to participate in sex that I really don't want or expect to enjoy because I have internalized some bad social messages about my sexual duties as a spouse. This would be consensual sex but not really an expression of my agency. Conversely, I might be having sex out of my own agency and even really enjoying it, but if I haven't communicated to my partner that this is what I want to be doing, and made sure that it's what they want to be doing, then the sex is not consensual. That's because *consensuality* is a feature of our *joint* activity; it's about how we are relating to and communicating with one another, whereas I can be acting with agency even if I am not communicating or coordinating well with another person. Both agency and consensuality are ethical prerequisites for sex.

In everyday speech, to *give consent* is to freely agree to something that someone else requests or proposes—a medical treatment, the terms of a contract, the display of our photograph, a kiss—with reasonably good information about what you are agreeing to. Philosophers, lawyers, sex educators, and others argue at length about exactly what consent is, and many have tried to build a richer concept of consent that encompasses more than just agreeing to something. For example, some philosophers and sex educators have tried to reimagine consent as a collaborative project. But I will stick to the more everyday meaning of the term, and nothing fancier or subtler. So, to give consent to sex, or to some sexual activity, is to explicitly agree to participate in it. You might have consensual sex without there being an explicit moment at which you say that you agree to it. You might consent to sex, and then the sex might stop being consensual if you stop communicating your willingness to participate, for instance, by going very limp and quiet and ceasing to engage or reciprocate. So, giving consent is neither necessary nor sufficient for having consensual sex. And consensual sex is not the same as good sex.

Our conversations about sexual agency and sexual ethics, however, have long tended to revolve around this moment of giving consent. The primary concern, in these conversations, has been with making sure that someone gives consent before proceeding with sex. This traditional conception of consent has shaped our sexual imagination. A central theme of this book is that this traditional consent framework is limiting and distorting when it comes to understanding good sex and how to enable it. This is so in several ways:

1. *The Dominance of Consent:* One often hears that "consent is everything" when it comes to sex, and in many contexts, consent is the only ethical tool that we are given for navigating sex. But traditional consent does not guarantee that sex will be good or pleasurable. We can freely agree to sex that we don't really want or want for bad reasons. We can agree to painful sex, embarrassing sex, boring sex, alienating sex, and depressing sex. I might agree to do something that I find demeaning or unpleasantly painful, perhaps because I would rather have bad sex than no sex at all, or because my partner isn't interested in finding out what would give me pleasure. Consent is also not enough to make sex ethically acceptable: Sex can be degrading, traumatizing, or a betrayal of someone else, for

instance, even when it is consensual. Too much focus on consent as the key to good sex keeps us from exploring all these other nuances. Think of the case of Aziz Ansari, the comedian who, in 2018, was publicly accused on babe.net of sexual misconduct by a woman he dated, pseudonymously known as Grace. Grace claimed that Ansari missed social cues, did not make it easy for her to leave his apartment, and moved too fast, with little attention to her desires, comfort, or pleasure. The public debate over this case turned, as it always does, into an argument over whether Grace had consented to the things she did with Ansari. (For instance, five days after the accusations came out, *Time* magazine published an article entitled, "The Aziz Ansari Allegation has people talking about 'affirmative consent.' What's that?") The implication was that if Ansari did nothing to Grace without her consent, then he had not done anything wrong. But consent does not seem like what went wrong here; it is not the most interesting thing to talk about. Ansari was thoughtless, selfish, and manipulative; bad at communicating and negotiating (as it seems Grace was too); and uninterested in what would give Grace pleasure or let her express her agency. We can understand this as a bad and disrespectful sexual encounter without pinpointing anything he did to her without her consent.

2. *The Flattening of Sexual Communication:* Consent is about agreeing to sexual activity and touch. But much of our good sexual communication isn't about asking for sex or agreeing to it. The kind of communication that leads to good sex includes not just yes-or-no questions like "May I do this

to you?" but also questions such as "What do you think it might be fun to do together?" "Is there anything you have always fantasized about doing?" and "Are there some things that just freak you out that you'd like to take off the table?" Beyond asking questions, I might begin to articulate a fantasy with someone, suggest a possibility that I think might please them, or seek help in exploring how I feel about an activity. None of this talk fits into a request-and-consent-or-refuse model of sexual communication.

3. *Sex as an Asymmetric Encounter Between Active Men and Passive Women*: The consent framework presupposes an asymmetrical situation in which one person asks for sex and the other agrees (or refuses). But surely, we hope that sexual negotiation will be more mutual and active than this! Agreeing to something that someone else has proposed is an extremely passive and minimal way to exercise one's agency. And in practice, given cultural realities, our discussions of consent almost always position a man as the one actively requesting sex and a woman as the one who agrees to or refuses it. When we see either "'No' means no!" or "'Yes' means yes!" we almost always imagine a woman saying "No!" or "Yes!" Feminist philosopher of sex Manon Garcia, in her 2023 book *The Joy of Consent*, points out that consent is almost always presented as a woman's concern: "It is presumed that men always want sex and are always in the position of proposing it, while women receive and vet proposals, accepting some and rejecting others." The idea that saying "yes" is the ultimate expression of women's sexual agency grows out of a picture within which women

are passive, with limited sexual imaginations. It reduces their sexual agency to the minimal act of allowing or disallowing the use of their bodies for someone else's desires and plans. It makes their own sexual pleasures and desires irrelevant.

4. *The Invisibility of Men's Sexual Needs and Vulnerabilities*: Meanwhile, it is rare that we even talk about men's sexual consent, not to mention their sexual agency more broadly. Within the traditional asymmetrical consent framework, men need to win or extract sexual permission from women, whose default attitude is refusal. Traditional consent discussions give us no tools for thinking about what sexual vulnerability and agency look like for men (not to mention for queer couples). We generally just assume that men always want sex and are the ones asking, so they don't need to consent, and because consent is "everything," this means that we don't need to worry about sexual harm to men or about enabling their agency or promoting their sexual pleasure. Our history of assuming that men are always ready and willing to have sex, and that their boundaries and vulnerabilities and the specifics of their desires don't matter, has done a lot of damage, as we will see later.

5. *The Focus on Permission and Restraint:* Most contemporary philosophers define consent as releasing someone from the obligation not to do something to you. We all have a right not to be sexually touched without our permission. When you consent to be touched, you waive that right. But it is rather bleak to think of this kind of waiving of a right not to be touched as the core of sexual negotiation. Ideally, we want people to

be actively seeking sex, not just willing to give up their right not to be touched. This definition of consent as giving someone permission not to restrain themselves from touching you makes it sound like we all just walk around holding ourselves back from "doing sex to one another." While there are all kinds of reasons to refrain from sex, I'd rather not understand restraint and refusal as our basic default way of interacting with one another.

6. *The Problem of Ongoing Consent*: Traditional consent discussions focus on how sex is *initiated*. We are told never to start any activity without the agreement of our partners. But sexual agency requires self-determination throughout a sexual encounter, not just at the start. While people have started talking about "ongoing consent" to reflect this reality, it is hard to see how this translates into practice within the traditional framework. The Antioch Policy was a set of strict rules for ensuring consent established by students at Antioch College in 1991. It was a list of fifteen rules, which made formal, affirmative verbal consent a requirement for each stage of a sexual encounter. In other words, according to the protocol, you had to explicitly ask permission for each new kind of touch or sexual activity. Although it was important in its early emphasis on affirmative consent throughout a sexual encounter, it was widely ridiculed for being too formulaic and exacting. Not only is such a protocol not sexy or practical, but it is unclear how often and when we are supposed to be asking; if I roll over slightly and lean against a different part of your belly, do I need to ask anew for consent? Should lovers just keep

asking one another constantly whether they agree to proceed? A sexual encounter organized around a series of requests and agreements would be awfully stilted. Moreover, we need to be able to do more than just keep requesting and consenting during sex. We should check in with our partners, not just by finding out if they still consent, but by exploring what would make them happy, asking questions such as, "Are you comfortable in this position?" or "Is there anything else that would feel good right now?"

The social myth that sexual ethics reduce to consent, and that consent is simple, is exemplified in a popular 2015 YouTube video called "Consent: It's as Simple as Tea." The video compares initiating sex to offering tea, making points such as: If someone says they want tea but then changes their mind, don't force them to still have tea! Unconscious people don't want tea! Just because you make tea, you are not entitled to make someone drink it! If someone starts to drink tea but doesn't finish it, don't force them to finish! Just because someone wants tea once doesn't mean they want tea constantly! The video ends with the slogan, "Consent is everything." It's a cute video, and effective at undercutting some especially pernicious talking points of rape culture. But, as others have pointed out, the tea analogy is distorting in its simplicity. Consent is not everything—it's not even everything for tea. Surely it matters whether you are drinking good tea, tea that you like, in a place that makes you happy to have tea, and not just whether you consented to drinking it. The tea analogy reinforces the asymmetrical model, with one person offering the tea and the other person accepting or rejecting it. It also makes it sound as if sexual communication is a simple negotiation: Do you want it or don't you, or maybe at most, what kind of tea do you want (although tellingly, in the video, no one is offered any range of tea options, just tea or no tea). And while we often drink tea together, it is not really a joint activity, so once someone says "yes" to tea, we just let them do their thing and drink it how they want; there isn't coordination or collaboration involved.

Our traditional thinking about consent is bound up with other culturally pervasive ideas around capitalism, heterosexuality, gender, and pleasure. Pseudonymous author Thomas MacAulay Millar, in his brilliant 2008 essay "Toward a Performance Model of Sex," writes,

> We live in a culture where sex is not so much an act as a thing: a substance that can be given, bought, sold, or stolen, that has a value and a supply-and-demand curve. In this "commodity model," sex is like a ticket. . . . Women are guardians of the tickets; men apply for access to them. This model pervades casual conversation about sex: Women "give it up," men "get some."

Men can "purchase" sex, either literally, or with promises of financial security, relationship commitments, and the like, or they can trick or manipulate women into giving it away. On this model, consent is about giving permission to someone to use your property, and rape is about using someone's property without permission. Women, for their part, need to preserve the value of their sexuality. If they give it away for free or too cheaply, they are sluts who are wasting their precious commodity. Like a car, the value of women's sexuality degrades with wear, which is why virginity is important and multiple partners are bad. Saving sex for marriage is basically holding onto an investment to make it as valuable as possible; after all, many women trade it for a dia-

16   SEX BEYOND "YES"

mond eventually. As Christian minister Josh McDowell puts it in his book, *Why Wait?*, which is designed to talk teens into abstinence, "Your body is a savings account to give to your mate as a wedding present, not to be spent on anything else." Monogamy seems like the only natural choice in this model, since once you own something, you rarely want to let others use it and put wear and tear on it.

This is an intensely depressing model of sex. It is an adversarial model in which the male "giver" and the female "receiver" are set up from the start as having conflicting interests and needing to reach a deal. It makes no room for women's pleasure or for queer sex. The idea that women lose rather than gain something when they have sex, and hence must be compensated, is a terrible path to sexual fulfillment.

Millar suggests that we instead understand sex on a *performance model*. Sex should not be understood as a transactional exchange of goods, he argues, but rather as a collaborative activity that we perform joyfully together, adjusting to one another's needs and rhythms, like a dance or a jazz improvisation. He writes, "Because it centers on collaboration, a performance model better fits the conventional feminist wisdom that consent is not the absence of 'no,' but affirmative participation. Who picks up a guitar and jams with a bassist who just stands there? Who dances with a partner who is just standing and staring? In the absence of affirmative participation, there is no collaboration." In such a performance, it is not enough that the participants say "yes" to participating. Everyone has to actually *do stuff*, or no performance will happen. In a dance or a jam, we don't just allow someone to use us, we express ourselves, in and through our collaboration with others. It makes no sense to "take" a collaborative performance from someone; rape, on the performance model, becomes less like a theft and more like a hostage situation. The more we practice, the better we become at doing stuff together. Many of us have a favorite dance partner, and there is something special about dancing with someone you've practiced with many times and whose moves you understand, someone with whom it has become easy to dance well. Some people are more comfortable sticking to that one favorite partner. But if you enjoy dancing with lots of people, there is no ethical reason not to have as many dance partners as you like.

Honestly, I don't love Millar's term "performance." As my students often point out, it makes it sound like sex is something we do primarily for the gaze of others, as though we are being evaluated on how well we do it. Calling it the collaborative model of sex might work better, though that sounds a little business-like. Regardless of terminology, I love Millar's idea of sex as an improvisation that we perform *together*. The performance model does a better job than the commodity model at helping us understand what sex is like when it goes well and joyfully. Neither the commodity model nor the performance model is the "accurate" or "correct" one. Both are metaphorical frames for thinking about sex, and not all sex is alike. But the commodity model dominates our cultural imagination, norms, and institutions, especially in traditional heterosexual contexts.

An important theme of this book is that sexual agency requires good scaffolding. *Scaffolding*, literally speaking, is a structure designed to strengthen and support something from the outside. Typically, scaffolding is designed to be temporary or modifiable, to be adjusted as the internal strength and stability of the thing being scaffolded changes. Scaffolding can be effective or ineffective; New Yorkers famously enjoy mocking the ugly scaffolding in their city, which remains on buildings for years and accomplishes nothing. But *good scaffolding* is a complex structure that gives something strength and stability by supporting it from multiple directions simultaneously, surrounding it with an intricate protective frame.

18   SEX BEYOND "YES"

Agency, specifically including sexual agency, needs good scaffolding. We are rarely fully self-determining—able to express and fulfill our needs, choices, and desires all on our own. Rather, our agency usually depends on a variety of social and interpersonal structures that hold it in place. When we act, choose, and express ourselves, we do so not just as isolated individuals, but as people embedded in social communities and contexts that can help us or hinder us. How much scaffolding we need to support our sexual agency and of what sort varies from person to person, activity to activity, and situation to situation, and the scaffolding we receive can be more or less effective. Someone who lives in a society in which a wide variety of sexual possibilities and orientations are accepted and openly discussed will have more opportunities for choice and pleasure open to them; this is community scaffolding. Someone who lives in a city with a good twenty-four-hour public transportation system can take more sexual risks, such as going home with someone new, because they can be confident that they can leave safely and easily whenever they choose to; this is physical scaffolding. Someone who received good sex education in school and has access to contraception and sexual health care is more empowered in their sexual choices than someone who does not have these things; this is institutional and educational scaffolding. Conversely, bad scaffolding—such as limited or misleading sex education, repressive sexual norms, or a legal system unfriendly to victims of sexual violence—undercuts our agency. We might think of this scaffolding as the *infrastructure* of sexual agency: the laws, physical systems and environments, community resources, and educational institutions that a society provides that support or undermine people's sexual agency. I prefer the term "scaffolding" to "infrastructure," because it highlights the way that *each of us individually* has specific support needs that *fluctuate over time*, while infrastructure is typically more collective and permanent.

Philosophers draw a distinction between *negative freedom*, which is freedom from being forced or coerced to do things you don't want to do, and *positive freedom*, which is the freedom *to* do things. If no one bothers me or forces me to do anything, but I have no real resources or skills and can't really do much, that isn't the kind of meaningful freedom I want. In my life, I want not only freedom *from* assault, incarceration, restrictions on my speech, and the like, but also the freedom *to* travel across borders, form relationships with whomever I want, build the kind of family I want, express my opinions and creativity in public space, and so forth. Such freedom requires scaffolding in the form of social support and resources: education, money, and a community that feeds me ideas and helps foster my creativity. Sexual agency is the same. A full-bodied positive freedom lets us try a wide variety of things, experience different kinds of relationships, test our boundaries, pursue our desires, and explore our pleasures and fantasies. This requires good social scaffolding. Building a social world in which sexual agency and pleasure can flourish requires changing our social practices and resources, not just teaching people to say and respect "no" and "yes"!

In the messy and imperfect social world in which we live, sex is often, maybe even usually, not a tidy affair. We are caught up in vexed social norms and power relationships; we are frail beings who become drunk and forgetful; we are frequently unsure of what we want. And yet we often manage to find sexual joy and agency anyhow, despite all this messiness. In a legal context, we may just need to focus on consensuality, that is, on whether sex was voluntary for all concerned and whether everyone involved knew that. But outside of the context of law, in which everything must be black or white, the reality is that sexual interaction is often complex, multidimensional, and murky. My goal is to explore how we can do our best at promoting and preserving sexual agency and pleasure in this world of compromises, vulnerabilities, and imperfections. This is a book about how to have good sex—sex that fulfills, excites, and empowers us, and leaves everyone feeling respected—amidst the mess and the ambiguity.

CHAPTER 2

Sex Talk

✖   ✖   ✖   ✖   ✖   ✖   ✖

You and your friend are traveling together in a new city, and you decide to take a long walk to explore. As you go, you say things to one another such as "Hey, that's a cool looking alley, let's take a detour down it, okay?" "Hmm, this street is kind of boring and trafficky, not as good to walk on as we thought it would be, let's pick another route," "Can we stop in this bookstore for a few minutes?" "Let's find a nice place to stop for a coffee break," and, importantly, "I'm getting tired and my feet are starting to hurt, can we jump on the subway and go home soon?" Unless you are especially passive-aggressive and a bad communicator, you don't just hope that your friend will pick up on your subtle body language if you eye that appealing alley or coffee shop longingly or start performatively limping a bit to indicate that you want to go home. You won't start your walk by saying, "Will you take a walk with me?" and then just assume that if your friend says "yes," they are stuck with whatever kind of walk comes next for however long you feel like walking. Instead, you set some loose provisional goals with your walking partner in advance. You agree that you have a few hours free to walk, and that you would like to explore a particular neighborhood and get lunch somewhere on the way, although you can always change that plan if something more fun pops up or if the original plan turns out to be less fun than you expected. It makes sense to tell your friend from the start if there's a gallery or a taco truck you've really been wanting to make it to, or if you have an injury that means you need to walk a little more slowly than usual.

It would be bizarre to think that such conversations kill the vibe of the walk. It would also be bizarre to spend the walk barking formal requests and permissions at one another and imposing a lot of rules: "Are you willing to turn left here?" "No!"; "No walking after sundown!" "Okay!"; "Can we keep walking?" "Yes!" This kind of rigid exchange of requests and responses is not how we enjoy a walk together. But that doesn't mean that we should walk in silence! All this talking—setting some goals, making some suggestions as you go, maybe mentioning some constraints, checking in, adjusting, building a rhythm and a route together, making sure both of you are still happy to keep walking— helps the walk be a good and interesting joint activity.

Likewise, good sex often involves a lot of talk. When we have sex, we want to be able to set some shared expectations but also explore some surprise alleys and stop for some unplanned treats along the way. There is an idea in broad circulation that a lot of talk leading up to or during sex is burdensome, because it is unsexy, or breaks the flow. But this idea is rooted in the traditional consent framework: People imagine that chatty sex would consist of constant requests, consents, and refusals. This would indeed be super annoying and unsexy! If you're finding that talking before and during sex kills the mood, you need to practice your sexy talking skills, not just stay quiet and hope for the best. A lot of our communication leading up to and during sex is not verbal, and this is appropriate: We use our bodies and our eyes to invite, to show pleasure and displeasure, to suggest, and more. I am interested in *all* the communication that goes on around sex, but talking is an integral part of that, and talking is far from inherently unsexy.

This chapter is about *sexual negotiation*: all the communication—both verbal and nonverbal—that goes into feeling out, exploring, and settling whether sex is going to happen and how it is going to go. "Negotiating" can involve driving a bargain, bartering, or compromising, and indeed a lot of bad sexual negotiation goes this way. The traditional consent model, which emphasizes "getting" consent out of a passive target of interest, encourages this kind of negotiation, which can result in manipulation, coercion, or misunderstanding. But negotiating can also involve finding your way together, figuring out how to jointly proceed in a manner that is responsive to the complexities of the situation—just as we negotiate the metro system in a new city, or a new friendship, or new parenthood. Good negotiation is a matter of successful collaborative co-navigation. Sexual negotiation, when it goes well, gets us to a point where we both understand how to give one another pleasure and respect one another's agency and boundaries. Not all good sexual negotiation ends in sex; it may turn out, once we communicate, that sex with one another is not what we want, at least not here and now.

At Winter Fire, an annual kink convention in Washington, DC, over half a dozen ninety-minute seminars on offer cover different dimensions of sexual negotiation before, during, and after various kinds of sex. All these seminars remind participants that consent is important, in the sense that everyone involved in any sexual encounter needs to communicate that they are participating willingly. But this is just the starting point. These seminars cover everything from how to

24   SEX BEYOND "YES"

ask for something when one is in a submissive role without breaking the eroticism of the encounter; to how to tell when your partner wants to stop an encounter; to how to explore your own and your partner's limits and interests; to how to use and read body language to communicate when your mouth is otherwise occupied.

Having learned from kink communities for years, I've developed a long list of the kinds of things people might negotiate, other than mere consent. Before you start having sex, you and your partner might explore questions such as: What are your hard limits? What are your provisional limits that you may be interested in pushing if the moment is right? What are your fantasies? How spontaneous do you want this sexual encounter to be—do you want to plan out a whole elaborate scene and specify in advance what you want to do, or do you want to leave some things open? What is your safe word? What toys do you like? What do you want to feel during this encounter—naughty; adventurous; safe; loved? What do you like to do right after sex—do you like to cuddle, talk, or be left alone? You might also promise one another not to cross various boundaries, or to stop when signaled. Once you are in the middle of things, you or your partner might ask, "Are you enjoying this right now? Do you want to go further, or do you want to stop?" You might remind your partner that it is okay to say "No more!" at any time.

Negotiation might also include *communicating about how you communicate*. You might want to ask, before you have sex with someone, how do they show pleasure? How do they act when they are feeling uncomfortable or unhappy? Perhaps you might want to explain to your partner that if you laugh during sex, it probably means that you're feeling awkward. Or that you often cry when you come, but not necessarily because you're unhappy. You and a prospective partner might want to talk about your shared ethics of sex: For instance, do you find all kinds of power play and domination abhorrent, or is that sometimes hot for you? Not every sexual encounter requires *all* these conversations. But in different circumstances, different kinds of conversations can help create a framework within which everyone can explore and express themselves safely.

At this point, you might be thinking that only kinky people and people who are having "edgy" sex need to worry about such things. If you enjoy only *vanilla* sex—that is, traditional, not especially kinky sex with one person in the context of a monogamous relationship—do you really have to talk about all this stuff? Can't you just assume that what your partner wants to do are "normal" things, and that as long as you're both being "normal," no big discussion is required? While there may well be less to negotiate with a long-time partner who you know is into a narrower range of activities, this way of thinking leads to a lot of bad sex. When vanilla sex partners rarely or minimally negotiate, they may think that if a "normal" activity is not that fun for them, then the problem is with them, and there's not much to be done about it. Multiple studies show that heterosexual women are routinely frustrated by sex and often don't know how to have an orgasm or what turns them on. People rarely think to ask heterosexual men whether they enjoy the sex they have, but I suspect they are often bored and frustrated as well and unable to explore fantasies or activities they might find pleasurable. When two people assume that only a narrow repertoire of activities is on the table, *and* when they are bad at talking about when and how they want to have sex, this is a recipe for boring, unfulfilling sex that may often be experienced as an imposition. Getting good at sexual negotiation takes skill and practice. Traditional heterosexual couples who have never really been forced to think reflectively about their sexual practices and desires may not have had the chance to develop these skills.

Why is it so tricky and complex to communicate well about sex?

First, sex is a domain of intense vulnerability and risk for most of us. It is easy to feel rejected or embarrassed, or to find yourself stuck doing something you really don't want to do, in a way that may be uncomfortable or even traumatizing. Many people have been raised to think that there are all sorts of moral restrictions on sex, so exercising their sexual agency and enjoying sexual pleasure can feel like a moral risk as well. A lot is at stake in sexual communication!

Second, erotic talk tends to be metaphorical, stagey, elliptical, connotative, and rich with innuendo. Realistically, this is part of what makes it sexy. But this can also make it hard to master and to interpret. When we are flirting or having sex, we often enter a kind of alternative language frame, in which nonliteral, indirect speech is the norm. When we role-play during sex, this shift to a nonliteral context is explicit. But more generally, we don't take phrases like "Tear me open!" as literal requests. When someone shouts out, "Who's your Daddy?" during sex, their partner doesn't provide their father's name. We teach young people that "'No' means no." But in many sexual contexts, this really isn't so. Someone might moan "No, no, no!" during an intense encounter involving consensual pain and submission, for instance, and this might very well be part of the erotic dynamic and not a call to stop. The much more complicated truth is that good, ethical sex requires successful skills at telling when "no" does and doesn't mean no, and more generally at interpreting loaded, indirect, and metaphorical speech.

Sexual negotiation, then, is marked by a tension: We need communication to be clear and successful because the stakes are high, and yet direct communication is often unsexy and inadequate to the nuances we want to express. We are not born knowing how to navigate this social and linguistic complexity, but we do have to learn to be good at it.

When we talk to each other about sex, or about anything really, we don't just need to think about which topics we are covering; we also need to think about what kinds of things we are *doing* with our speech—what kind of action are we performing by speaking? Putting aside sex for a moment, imagine that I say to you, "You can take the train to New York from here." Now imagine instead that I ask you, "Can you take the train to New York from here?" Or that I say, "If I were you, I'd take the train to New York from here." Or, finally, that I order you: "Take the train to New York from here!" These four communications are about the same topic, and they use almost the same words, but they have very different *force*—they do completely different things. One conveys information, one asks a question, one gives advice, and one tells you what to do. Philosophers call the study of how we use language to do different things and shape our social interactions differently *speech act theory*.

I think a little bit of speech act theory can be useful for sorting through some of the nuances of good and bad sexual negotiation. During sexual negotiation, the force of our speech makes a big difference to how things go and to whether we are treating one another well. *Requesting*, *consenting*, and *refusing* are only a few of the things we can do with language in sexual negotiation. We can also, for instance, *invite* one another to do things, *suggest* sexy ideas, *warn* our partner about our triggers, *ask* about a partner's preferences, and *order* people to do things. All these different kinds of linguistic actions—or *speech acts* as philosophers call them—accomplish different social tasks and call for different kinds of response. I might be quite happy for you to invite me to kiss you, but I may feel violated if you order me to do so.

28 SEX BEYOND "YES"

Promising is a special type of speech act, which the promiser uses to bind their own actions and make themselves accountable. Before I agree to bondage play with you, I might want you to promise that if you tie me up so that I can't get away, under no circumstances will you tickle me. That promise might be the condition under which I am willing to be tied up. Your promise keeps me safe, and it also enables us both to do something that we want to do but otherwise wouldn't be able to do. If you say, "I don't plan to tickle you," or "Tickling people is not usually my mood," this *predicts* that you won't tickle me, but what I may need is the serious *promise*, which sets up an obligation and accountability. Some people think that sexual promises are never appropriate because we shouldn't control one another's sexual activities by binding our future choices. But promises not to cross limits can be crucial tools for making it possible for people to feel comfortable doing things they otherwise wouldn't be willing to do.

Ordering someone to do something sexual is almost always wrong (unless it's within a negotiated kinky domination encounter): Orders make refusal difficult; they put the person pursued in the position of having to be defiant if they want to refuse. And although the traditional consent framework focuses on requests for sex, requesting sex can also create pressure to accept. Granting a request is a favor, so refusing a request can seem ungenerous: Why are you unwilling to do me this favor? Sometimes, requesting sex is appropriate. I might say to my partner, "Hey, I know we've both been really busy lately, but will you please have sex with me tonight?" In the context of a long-term, healthy relationship, that might be totally fine, but it's definitely not maximally sexy. And if someone I don't know well or haven't slept with before *requests* that I have sex with them, I am likely to be pretty put off. A request calls for a favor, and it is odd and uncomfortable to ask for sex as a favor from a stranger. Conversely, I don't typically want someone to sleep with me as a favor; I would rather they slept with me out of their own desire. And so, I try to avoid requesting sex. What then are other ways in which we initiate sex, and, especially, what are ways to do it well?

A lot of good sex starts with an *invitation* instead of a request. Invitations are welcoming without being demanding. If I say to you, "I'm cooking dinner at my place on Wednesday, please come, if you don't, I'll be hurt," then I am requesting your presence, not inviting you. Conversely, if I say to you, "I'm cooking dinner at my place on Wednesday and you can show up or not, it's totally up to you, I don't care either way," then this is also not really an invitation but perhaps more like an offer; at best it's a highly unwelcoming, inept invitation. A more apt invitation might be "I'd love to cook dinner for you on Wednesday if that sounds good to you!" Invitations leave the invitee free to accept or reject them. If you turn down my invitation, I get to be disappointed, but not aggrieved (although I can feel aggrieved if you turn it down rudely or insultingly). A sexual invitation makes clear that sex would be welcome. Notice that if I *invite* you to have sex with me, then consent and refusal are not even the right categories of speech acts when it comes to your response. You can accept an invitation, but it strains language to say that you consent to it, because you are not agreeing to a request.

There is an art to issuing good invitations. How do we welcome someone to do something with us while not pressuring them? When does it become appropriate to invite someone to do something? We face such social questions routinely, and not just in the sexual domain. If I meet a stranger on the bus and chat with them for two minutes about the traffic, it would be inappropriate for me to invite them to my wedding. Similarly, sexual invitations have their own social norms and ethical standards. I cannot invite you to have sex with someone other than me; this would be exploitative. It would be super uncomfortable for me to invite you to have sex with me at the end of a two-minute chat about the weather in the grocery line. I also cannot invite you to have sex with me if doing so would be an abuse of my power, or if it would otherwise be difficult for you to say no to the invitation. It isn't really an invitation if you aren't free to turn it down. Even though invitations can always be declined, this doesn't mean that it's okay to extend inappropriate invitations—which is something that street harassers, for instance, often don't seem to understand.

In most circumstances, an invitation is a much better way to initiate sex than a request. You want to welcome a partner into the possibility of sex, leaving them free to accept or reject, not pressure them into doing you a favor. Especially when we are just getting together with someone for the first time, whether for a casual hookup or at the start of a more serious relationship, sexual invitations are generally much more appropriate than requests.

Typically, when you invite me to do something and I accept, it is appropriate for us to both express gratitude. You thank me for coming to dinner, and I thank you for having me. In fact, if you invite me and I decline, it is still polite for me to express at least token gratitude for the invitation. But sex feels different; it seems odd to say that I owe someone gratitude for inviting me to have sex. I get "invited" to have sex every time I walk down a major street in workout clothes, and while I sometimes get called a "bitch" for not showing gratitude, I don't feel like I owe gratitude for these routine and unappealing invitations. Why are sexual invitations different in this way? First, many of them are inappropriate. Some random guy on the street shouldn't be inviting me to have sex as I walk by, and so his rude invitation doesn't require gratitude. But also, showing gratitude for a sexual invitation is often risky, especially for women. Men will often take a polite expression of gratitude as a reason to keep pursuing a woman, or to harass or hound her in order to try to get her to change her mind. I think that a totally appropriate sexual invitation (at the end of a date that seems to have gone well, say) does call for some expression of gratitude, whether one is interested in accepting or not—something along the lines of "I appreciate the offer, but it's not what I am feeling, sorry." But we live in a world filled with so many inappropriate sexual invitations, and so many men who refuse to take "no" for an answer if they sense any possible weakness or opening, that it's often a better plan not to express gratitude, even though it would be best if we could do so safely.

In an established, long-term relationship, sex is sometimes initiated via a different kind of speech act: a *gift offer*. A gift offer is a communicative act; the offer of a gift is part of sexual negotiation, and no gift offer need be accepted. Gifts, by nature, are designed to please their recipient (though they may fail to do so), and they are given out of generosity, not obligation. While it would be odd and almost always inappropriate to offer sex as a gift to someone we barely know, it's not unusual for longtime partners to offer each other gifts of sex, not as barters, but as generous attempts to give pleasure. I might offer my partner sex to cheer them up after a discouraging day, or to welcome them back from a trip, or to celebrate a milestone. Or I might offer to role-play or indulge a fetish that both of us know is not my "thing." Gifts, by nature, cannot be demanded; they must be freely given. In daily life, we are often compelled by etiquette or power relations to give gifts—to buy something off a registry for an annoying cousin who is getting married, or to contribute to the office gift for the boss. But these aren't really gifts; they are ways of discharging a social obligation. If you plead with me or order me to indulge some fetish of yours, then my doing so is not a gift.

Nothing is automatically troubling about offering to engage in a sexual activity with someone we care about out of generosity rather than direct desire. In fact, it is lovely to do things for people because we want to give them pleasure! This is one reason why I am not a fan of the enthusiastic consent model of sexual negotiation, which defines consensual sex partly in terms of enthusiasm. While enthusiasm is wonderful, we do not have to be enthusiastic about everything we do. Just because I am utterly unenthusiastic about going grocery shopping doesn't mean that I am going nonconsensually or that there is an ethical problem with me going, and I might decide to buy groceries for a sick friend as an act of generosity even though I do not find going to the grocery store thrilling. Some asexual people are never enthusiastic about sex but value sexual generosity within their relationships. While sex must always be freely chosen and never coerced, not all sexual encounters need be enthusiastically desired by everyone involved.

Our social norms around gift-giving are complex, and anthropologists have shown that gift exchanges play an important role in building and sustaining communities and relationships. Gifts call for reciprocation in every culture, despite plenty of other cultural variations in gifting practices. This is part of how they sustain relationships. Part of what is complicated about the norms of gift reciprocation is that they are open-ended. Reciprocating a gift *too quickly* or *too closely in kind* is usually a social norm violation: If you give me a book that you think I would love as a spontaneous gift, you should not expect me to immediately hand a different book back; it would be even more inappropriate for me to give you the same book back. The size, timing, and content of reciprocation must all be keyed subtly and not too directly to the original gift. If the reciprocation they call for is too specific, then they are no longer gifts but something more like barters. Accepted sexual gifts also create an obligation to reciprocate, though not immediately, or exactly in kind, or on any specific schedule. If you routinely indulge my sexual desires out of generosity, it is disrespectful and undermining of our relationship if I never reciprocate.

Sexual gifts, like sexual invitations, can be appropriate or inappropriate. Unsolicited dick pics are typically not appropriate gifts. If you are just getting to know someone, a sexual gift offer is typically presumptuous: You aren't yet in a position to impose an obligation upon them to reciprocate. But generous offers of sexual gifts, designed first and foremost to please one's partner rather than to directly satisfy one's own sexual desires, are a normal part of a healthy long-term relationship. An authentic, appropriate, and thoughtful sexual gift offer within a relationship calls for an expression of gratitude. But we are under no obligation to accept offers of sexual gifts even when they are appropriate.

Public discussions of sex and consent are typically focused on how sex starts. But our ability to have real control over when we want to stop sexual activity is every bit as important to our sexual agency as our ability to control whether and when we start it. Sex is self-determining and ethical only when everyone involved understands the exit conditions and can stop when they want, and everyone knows and trusts that they can do this, without punishment, humiliation, or other harm. This general idea is familiar from the domain of medical care: We each have the right not only to choose whether to start a treatment, but also whether and when to stop it. But we haven't spent much time discussing how important it is to be able to effectively control when a sexual encounter ends.

34 SEX BEYOND "YES"

A fascinating and powerful tool for scaffolding easy exits is a prenegotiated *safe word*. When used well, a safe word provides a framework that allows everyone to understand when someone wants to exit a sexual activity. A safe word can be a random distinctive word (one friend uses "kimchi" and another uses "Helsinki"). Participants can also use a "green," "yellow," and "red" system, which allows for more nuance. Saying "green" reassures your partner that everything is going well and indicates active enjoyment and a desire to continue. Calling "red" ends the sexual encounter. It retracts consent and shifts the participants out of the sexual context back into the everyday. Saying "yellow" indicates discomfort or wariness, calling on the other person to be on the lookout for signs that their partner wants to shift gears a bit or stop the activity. It is important that safe words be contextually irrelevant words that are not going to otherwise come up in the sexual encounter, but rather break into it unambiguously.

Safe words allow people to do activities, explore desires, and experience pleasures that would be too risky otherwise. They expand the space of opportunities for sexual agency. Safe words let someone exit an activity at any time without having to explain themselves or accuse anyone of transgression or any other kind of wrongdoing (although they can also be used when there has been a transgression). Calling "red" does not imply that anyone has messed up, it calls for no apology and requires no apology after its use. Some people act hurt after their partner has used their safe word, or they try to argue with them or demand reasons. But these are violations of the established linguistic norms of safe words. Establishing safe words lets participants decide together how to make the boundaries of a sexual encounter clear. Even if never used, they serve a powerful function in creating the scaffolding within which activities can happen.

Sometimes when I talk about the importance of safe words, I am asked, why isn't it enough for everyone to just respect the phrase "No, let's stop"? Would we need safe words if we just listened to and respected one another? Don't only inconsiderate people need safe words? Safe words are especially useful in nonliteral contexts where "no" may not mean no and "stop" may not mean stop. But such contexts aside, there are many social barriers against shouting "no" or "stop" at someone in the middle of sex, perhaps especially if we like them and care about their feelings and might want to have sex with them in the future. Women in particular are socialized not to say "no" directly or often. A direct request to stop almost inevitably creates a rift in an interaction that then needs repairing. It's difficult for such a speech act not to come off as a confrontational rebuke. It also opens the door to counterarguments for why there is actually no need to stop. A safe word is, *by explicit negotiation* and tradition, a *clean* break.

Safe words should never be the *only* way that someone can exit a scene or activity—all participants need to remain flexibly responsive to other cues as well. So, "Oh no, please, I can't take any more, no!" might well be part of a consensual domination scene rather than an attempt to end it, but "No really, get off me, you are pressing on my bladder" is almost always an indication that consent has been withdrawn, as is "Damn it, it's already 8:00—I need to leave for work." Safe words are a tool for enhancing sexual autonomy and safety, but they should never replace sensitivity to other verbal and nonverbal cues that someone wants to stop an encounter.

I'm a huge fan of safe words. I think they should have a dramatically larger role in our culture than they do. Imagine if teenagers were taught from the start in sex education classes that establishing a safe word is a standard part of good sex. This could be so empowering and comforting during an early, fumbling sexual encounter, when young people don't yet really know what they are doing or what they like. Anyone could call their safe word if they were uncomfortable, rather than trying to have a conversation in the middle of an already-awkward, already-anxious sexual encounter about how the other person did nothing wrong and shouldn't feel bad, but really shouldn't try to pressure or encourage them to continue, and so on. Indeed, I would love to see the youngest of children taught about safe words in a non-sexual context, giving them a tool to communicate when they need to exit a situation, whether or not they have the words or presence of mind to explain why. While children cannot say "no" to anything they like, they can be taught in which circumstances prenegotiating a safe word makes sense and how to use them. Children should be able to safe word out of hugs from relatives, scary movies, tickling games, birthday parties, foods that they don't feel comfortable eating, and other things that threaten their sense of bodily safety and control but that they may want to try.

Sexual negotiation is multidimensional and complex, and there is lots of room for subtlety. The language we use and the force with which we speak can help sex go well and protect everyone's agency. Being willing to hear and respect our partners' "no" or "yes" is not nearly enough. We all have a responsibility to protect and promote our partners' self-determination and pleasure, and we all benefit from being able to express our own needs and desires well. This means we should learn to be adept at the full range of sexual communication.

CHAPTER 3

Scaffolding Good Sex

✳   ✳   ✳   ✳   ✳   ✳   ✳

J ean is a nineteen-year-old man who is attracted to other men. He lives
in a strict religious community within which homosexuality is viewed
as a sin worthy of exile, in a country where homosexuality is still treated as a
serious crime. He has had no sex education and finds his own desires confusing and unclear, but he does not dare discuss them with anyone. He strikes up
a friendship with Guy, a local twenty-two-year-old man. Guy has had some
experience with gay sex and suggests to Jean that they should try having sex.
Jean is attracted to Guy, but he isn't sure what this would involve.

Jean is a nineteen-year-old man who is attracted to other men. He is trans,
and has only recently started living publicly as a man, and only in some contexts. His family and his high school friends don't know he is trans, and he
is not ready to come out to them. He lives in a fairly progressive city and has
several gay friends but no trans friends. He decides to go by himself to a local
queer sex party, presenting as a man. At the party, the hosts offer explicit
instructions for how to approach others and how to negotiate consent. But
this is a new kind of environment for Jean, and he is very nervous. He is

38   SEX BEYOND "YES"

shy about talking to anyone and doesn't know how to navigate revealing his anatomy to a potential partner. After several drinks, he strikes up a conversation with twenty-two-year-old Guy, who he suspects is flirting with him. Jean would like to try to initiate sex with Guy but isn't sure how.

Jean is a nineteen-year-old man who is attracted to other men. He has been seeing twenty-two-year-old Guy for several months. Jean grew up around queer people and both of them live in the same queer collective. The collective gets along great, although a few years ago one of the members was abusive toward two of the others. After a series of house meetings, the abuser was asked to leave, and the members of the collective worked to make sure that the victims had the support they needed to feel safe staying. Jean and Guy enjoy playing a game where they draw cards to see which sexy things they will do that night, although either of them can veto any card that comes up. Tonight, they have agreed they are both in the mood for playing with new rope that they bought together.

In each of these scenarios, Jean wants to have sex with Guy, and there is no reason to think that anyone is going to be pressured into anything nonconsensual. But Jean's sexual agency is quite different in each case.

In the first scenario, Jean's sexual agency is minimal. He is scared and ashamed and has no community support; he doesn't know how to articulate his desires; if anything goes wrong in a sexual encounter with Guy, the consequences could be catastrophic for him. For all these reasons, Jean's choices are limited, and he can't really safely negotiate the choices he does have. He also doesn't fully understand what he wants or what he can or can't do. His ability to make informed, safe, self-expressive decisions is severely compromised.

In the second scenario, Jean has some support for his agency, but his agency is still compromised in some ways. He is in a safer environment, and he has been given some helpful building blocks for figuring out and expressing what he wants. But he is inexperienced, and he doesn't really have a community in which he can be himself and get support. This undermines his confidence and leaves him vulnerable.

In the final scenario, Jean has close to maximal agency. He can figure out what he wants and communicate his desires effectively. He trusts his partner to respect his boundaries. He and his partner have built up good sexual communication over time. He has community support and plenty of role models, and he can be fairly confident that if anything goes wrong, he will remain safe.

The differences between these scenarios are not differences in Jean's internal capacity to make autonomous choices, nor in Guy's good will, nor even in Jean's desires. Rather, the differences are in the *scaffolding* that Jean's agency has. That is, in each case, Jean's communal, material, educational, legal, and interpersonal surroundings hold his agency in place poorly, or well. How much scaffolding he needs and of what kind depends on how fragile his agency is and in what ways. In the first scenario, the scaffolding he has is actively bad; his legal, educational, and community environment block his ability to understand his own desires or needs and put him at risk. In the second scenario, as a newly emerging, semi-closeted young trans man in an intense and alien environment, Jean needs more and different kinds of scaffolding than he would in other circumstances. In the final scenario, he is lucky enough to be in a supportive environment in which he is free to experiment and play, expanding his agency and sexual possibilities.

People never have sex as an isolated dyad (or triad, or whatever). All of us are always embedded in a *social ecology* that scaffolds some activities, experiences, and choices, and not others. Our sexual agency

40   SEX BEYOND "YES"

depends not just on what we and our partners say, but also on a wide range of features of our environment. Scaffolding might take the form of a policy, an educational program, a conversation, a building, or a friend group. The best communicators in the world cannot have strong sexual agency in a country with maximally restrictive and punitive sexual norms or laws, or when trapped in a brightly lit room in an institution, such as a prison or hospital, that offers no privacy. These are extreme examples, but none of us exercises our agency in a vacuum. How can good sex—sex that is pleasureful, ethical, and self-determining and self-expressive for everyone involved—be well-scaffolded?

Our physical environment scaffolds our sexual agency well or poorly. For example, I am much more able to take risks and explore sexual possibilities if I can easily leave if I want to. If I am trapped at someone's house and relying on them for a ride home, I have much less agency than if I am free to come and go as I please. I also have more sexual agency if I have privacy—my own room and a door that closes. How much sexual self-determination and choice do you have if you are homeless and will be harassed by the police or at least deeply embarrassed if you have sex in the public spaces available to you, where your very existence is already stigmatized? It virtually never occurs to city governments and social service providers to think about how to provide homeless people with safe, clean, dignified, and private spaces for sex. Economic scaffolding is closely related to physical scaffolding. If I have the money to pay for a cab home at any moment, or to quickly leave a partner who has become controlling and abusive, this enhances my agency. If I am financially dependent on a partner, it is much harder for me to stand up to their pressures or to explore my options.

Good sex education is one way to scaffold sexual agency well. Young people need to learn how to say what they want, not just what they don't want, and how to work together to enhance and protect one another's pleasure and agency. School systems and public health agencies should distribute high quality, inclusive information about sexual safety and sexual possibilities. Schools and other institutions that are responsible for sex education can design their curriculum around enhancing and protecting agency much more than they currently do. Teens and preteens can be given exercises that help them think about what would give them pleasure, and techniques for good negotiation, rather than just information about the various ways in which sex can be dangerous and the importance of saying and respecting "no." Such exercises and techniques should cover not only traditional sexual intercourse, but the full range of sexual activities—kissing, fingering, and so on—that younger teens are likely to engage in. Teens should learn about where it is and isn't safe to have sex; the importance of having a way to get home; how it may feel when your boundaries are being pushed too hard; how to talk to your partner about whether they have drunk too much to continue; how to invite someone into a sexual encounter, and how to respond to being turned down; and of course, how to find and use contraception and sexual health care. Sex education that teaches people with nonstandard bodies—such as disabled, trans, and intersex people—how to discover what is sexually pleasurable and empowering for them increases their sexual agency. In contrast, minimal or misleading sexual information obviously reduces sexual agency, as does education that hides or shames possibilities like queer sex and polyamorous sex. Florida's 2022 "Don't Say Gay" law, which bans any mention of queer sex in an educational setting, openly undermines sexual agency.

Neither conservative sex education, which focuses on preventing all teen sex, nor progressive sex education, which generally focuses on preventing rape, does anything to help young people understand the wide variety of sexual tastes, pleasure, and activities out there, or how to negotiate them respectfully and safely. Blocking potential abusers from succeeding is always important, but explaining only what can go wrong does not teach people how to make things go right. We should be encouraging self-exploration and self-reflection, as well as reading and discussion, that helps people figure out their boundaries, desires, fears, and limits.

Education that protects bodily agency needs to begin in early childhood, before it is appropriate to talk about sex explicitly. We should teach children that except in a serious emergency, they never have to agree to being touched or hugged by anyone, and that they should always make sure that someone wants to be touched before they touch them. While almost all of us need touch and affection, children are protected and empowered by learning that they have bodily integrity and that they are the ones who get to decide on their own boundaries. This doesn't mean teaching them that touch is bad, but rather that touching is a thing that should be pleasurable and self-expressive for everyone, not just endured out of social obligation. Right now, we go straight from teaching kids that their bodies are not their own, and that they have to give hugs or eat things on command or allow themselves to be picked up without warning, to expecting them to know how to negotiate consent and boundaries as teens. Teenagers generally need to unlearn early childhood messages to the effect that their bodily boundaries are not worthy of respect and that their physical desires and aversions don't matter when it comes to everyday interactions with family members and family friends. Likewise, it can also be confusing for kids who are not taught to check whether people want to be hugged or touched to suddenly be responsible for ensuring consent when they become teenagers.

Laws and policies also serve as scaffolding for sexual agency. The Antioch Policy was probably helpful scaffolding at the time, when explicit concern with consent was quite new, but now it feels like a clunky and constraining piece of scaffolding, and we have largely abandoned it. Effective institutional mechanisms for reporting sexual violations, supporting victims, and implementing restorative justice can protect sexual agency. A legal system that makes it easy for victims to receive a respectful hearing and creates a culture of accountability can help with both preventing sexual assault and allowing repair when it happens. A culture of accountability need not be a carceral or retributive culture. Indeed, over-punishing sexual offenders and stripping them of their basic rights and humanity may in fact weaken our actual culture of accountability by raising the bar unreasonably high for our willingness to bring sexual violation charges against someone and find them guilty.

Many of our institutions, including universities, legal systems, and workplaces, have formal and informal norms of confidentiality around sexual violations. Victims are not easily able to find one another to share stories and help put together a larger narrative, which can help them contextualize what happened. Often, victims must legally fight for the right to tell their own stories. For example, 2021 Australian-of-the-year Grace Tame, who was groomed and repeatedly assaulted as a teenager by her much older teacher, fought an extended legal battle for the right to speak publicly about her abuse so that she could counter media rumors that she had pursued the relationship herself and that it had been consensual. The institutional suppression of victims' voices helps perpetuate the myth that sexual assault is rare, and its victims are abnormal. Such cultures of confidentiality are isolating, disorienting, and disempowering and do not help future potential victims. They also

44 SEX BEYOND "YES"

corrode community trust by setting up cycles of gossip, half-truths, and suspicion.

Medical institutions can also scaffold or undermine sexual agency. They can support sexual agency, for example by providing contraception, abortion, and drugs like PrEP, which prevents HIV transmission, thereby increasing peoples' opportunities for pursuing sexual opportunities and pleasures. Conversely, the former categorization of homosexuality as a diagnosable "disease" made it harder for queer people to understand themselves as self-determining sexual agents, rather than as "compelled" by their "disordered" natures. This medicalization of homosexuality also smoothed the path to conversion "treatment" centers, which directly attack people's sexual agency and bodily integrity. More subtly, medical institutions have generally defined cis men's sexuality in terms of their ability to get and keep erections at will. The medicalization of so-called erectile dysfunction pathologized normal variations in men's sexual responses. Arguably, this has contributed to a sad narrowing of our cultural imagination for what cis men's sexual flourishing and agency might look like down to simply "getting and keeping it up," with little room left for more nuanced conversations about men's sexual well-being, desire, and fulfillment. Viagra fed into to the myth that men's desire for sex should be constant and context-free.

Communities can create or undermine conditions for their members' agency. They can offer support and acceptance for various kinds of relationships and give their members resources for self-understanding and self-determination. They can offer trust, inclusion, and safety—or isolation, scapegoating, secrecy, and bullying. Sexually active teenagers have to hide what they are up to if they know they will get in trouble from their parents or other community members. If they are in unsupportive communities, they may have minimal access to advice and understanding, and probably to sexual health care. This all makes it hard for them to stay safe, or to figure out what they enjoy and how they should expect to be treated, or to learn good sexual negotiation skills. Forcing relationships into secrecy denies people in those relationships easy, safe access to resources and advice. Queer people in homophobic communities are disproportionately dependent on their partners for support, and not easily able to leave relationships or to get outside checks on whether they are being mistreated; this was part of the problem for Jean and Guy in the first scenario at the beginning of this chapter. Socially isolated people who cannot turn to their community for support or for resources to understand their experiences are easily gaslit by partners with power over them into not knowing what they want, or not understanding the ways in which they are being sexually coerced or sexually short-changed.

Communities can provide scaffolding that helps their members try things out safely and determine their own sexual narratives. Strong, supportive communities allow their members to turn to others in the community for advice; provide inside information on who treats their partners well; serve as a source of collective stories and concepts that help members articulate and understand their desires and limits; and offer resources and help when something goes wrong. In contrast, unsupportive communities corrode sexual agency and self-determination. Community stereotypes about some people being "sluts," "whores," "frigid," "oversexed," "faggots," and so on, make members less able to determine their own narratives and build positive sexual identities. Communities that stigmatize some kinds of sex, or sex involving some kinds of people (disabled people, or older people, or trans people, for instance) straightforwardly undermine sexual agency. They reduce sexual opportunities for some groups of people and narrow people's imagination of what kinds of sexual pleasure are available.

Body shaming is deeply built into our culture; many people have bodies that are treated as fair game for mockery and expressions of disgust. Fat people and trans and intersex people, for instance, are consistent targets. It is obvious that body shaming is hurtful, but it also undermines sexual agency. Receiving the message that your body is inherently undesirable can make you feel like you are lucky to get any sexual attention at all, and thus not in a position to draw limits or reject sexual advances. Internalized shame can also directly interrupt a person's ability to take pleasure in their own body and its activities and to enjoy sex unselfconsciously. We don't have to pretend that we find every single body equally lovely and glorious, and we don't even have to adore our own body, but we should work to uproot cultural norms and tropes that label whole categories of bodies as unfuckable and shameful.

A vigorous debate rages over whether people are blameworthy for their sexual preferences. If your tastes just happen to re-create traditional axes of privilege and exclusion—if you're only attracted to thin, fit, able-bodied people of your own race, for instance—are you morally responsible for those tastes? We can't just decide, through an act of will, to change who we are attracted to. Certainly, as philosopher Amia Srinivasan has emphasized, no one ever *owes* anyone else sexual interest, no matter what. Someone may understandably be angry or frustrated that in our culture, very few people find bodies like theirs attractive. That doesn't mean that they are *entitled* to sexual attention or attraction from any particular person. Yet I don't think this lets us entirely off the moral hook when it comes to our own attractions. We can turn a critical eye toward the ideological and social training that has shaped our sexual tastes. We can work on trying to expand and retrain our sexual sensibilities. We cannot voluntarily and immediately determine our sexual attractions, but we can often partially shape our attractions over time, by being thoughtful about what spaces we move in and what media and messages we consume. Regardless of whether we succeed, there is *never* a good reason to shame or mock specific bodies or body-types. At the community level, we should collectively work to undermine and criticize stigmatizing images, tropes, and ideologies that shape people's desires in denigrating and exclusionary ways.

Social scripts are powerful cultural tools for shaping, expanding, and contracting sexual agency. They help us know which things it makes sense to do next in social situations. We have social scripts for how to order in a restaurant (get the menu, wait for the waitstaff to come back to the table, order drinks first or last depending on whether it is a fancy sit-down restaurant or a fast-food restaurant, etc.), how to write and respond to work emails, and much more. Following social scripts is not exactly *mandatory*, but it makes social coordination and interaction easier and more effective; it saves a huge amount of social energy; and it brings us social approval. The cost of violating scripts can be social retaliation, or just incomprehension. So, for the most part, we let social scripts set the blueprint for what we say and do in various circumstances. Scripts also guide us in separating "normal" from "deviant" behavior.

Heterosexual, vanilla sex tends to follow highly constrained scripts that involve quite little negotiation. Moreover, many of our scripts for this kind of sex tend to reduce everyone's agency and often especially disempower women. For instance, the scripts put men in the role of pursuing sex and women in the role of waiting to be asked, and they narrow women's options for meaningful refusal. Scripts like that of the guy who pluckily keeps trying to win the girl of his dreams are more specific variants of this basic trope. According to the standard hetero-

48   SEX BEYOND "YES"

sexual script, sex ends at male orgasm, ideally inside a vagina. Heterosexual scripts typically involve "a chain of events fully scripted and oriented towards men's pleasure," as Manon Garcia puts it in *The Joy of Consent*. Scripts of this sort do not allow for men to be uninterested in sex, while women are expected to walk a precarious line, resisting sex but ultimately being willing, but not too willing.

Garcia points out that our social scripts control which sexual activities need discussion and consent and which do not, and which scripts are activated will depend on context. For example, straight people generally assume that anal sex requires separate discussion and consent within a sexual encounter, but this is not usually true in gay male contexts. We cannot possibly explicitly negotiate every single motion we make; we need scripts to help set background social expectations so that we can discuss how we want to vary from them. But scripts can become dangerous when partners do not share an understanding of which ones they are following; or when the scripts are narrow and inflexible and thereby dramatically reduce agency; or when they are toxic and harmful to one or both partners.

Children and teenagers increasingly learn their first sexual scripts from internet pornography. The typical scripts disseminated by mainstream pornography are not only misogynist, but narrow and unrealistic, with poor norms of negotiation. If we mostly learn our sexual scripts this way, it will narrow our sexual imaginations and set up unhelpful and impractical standards for how to initiate and have sex. As my adult son put it to me recently, learning how to have sex by watching mainstream porn is like learning how to drive only through watching *Fast and Furious* movies. Simply telling preteens and teens that they are not allowed to watch internet porn, however, seems hopeless, given its accessibility and interest, and given that all teens love forbidden fruit. Telling kids that the porn they are seeing is "bad" and that sex shouldn't be like that also seems unhelpful if they have no other scripts easily available to them.

Many parents and educators worry that kids are learning how sex is supposed to go and what it is supposed to look like from porn. And yet these same parents and educators often show no interest in exposing teenagers to better or more diverse models of sex. Simply shielding teens from sexual content is neither realistic nor supportive of their agency. Porn on the internet is one of the great inevitabilities of the twenty-first century. Our best path is to give teenagers access to healthy and thoughtful alternatives to standard-issue porn, and to give them access to forums for critical discussion of what they are seeing. A whole world of alternative porn is out there, especially home-made porn featuring queer sex, creative sex, and sex between people who genuinely enjoy one another's bodies and company. No one thinks that helping teens find good porn is a good idea. But teaching them to read porn critically and to realize that narrow and formulaic sexual scripts limit their agency and pleasure is important. This is a better plan than pretending that we can shield them from any understanding of what sex looks like. Teens aside, it would be better if alternative and feminist pornography were more accessible, and big-budget traditional porn with its restrictive and toxic scripts were less accessible.

In a viral 2012 blog post, Amy Gahran introduced the concept of the *relationship escalator*. Gahran pointed out that traditional romantic relationships are supposed to follow a specific step-by-step, unidirectional script, ideally culminating in marriage, property ownership, and children. Steps along the way include flirting, starting sexual contact, committing to monogamy, making the relationship public, meeting one another's families, and moving in together. Couples are supposed to progress up the relationship escalator without moving backward, stalling, or stepping off, otherwise the relationship is not "going anywhere" and is a failure or a waste of time, according to the script. Scripts like this help to channel and coordinate our agency, but they also dramatically reduce it, by making actions that don't fit the scripts socially costly and hard to interpret. The relationship escalator script narrows the life paths available to us, and it also narrows our sexual agency more specifically by telling us that sex only belongs within a specific kind of narrative—there is no point to sex unless it is within a relationship that is "going somewhere" or has the potential to progress, according to this script.

We cannot invent new scripts out of thin air as the whole point of them is that they are *entrenched* patterns of social interaction that help carve out normal and expected behavior. In fact, scripts, including sexual scripts, are often built into the basic design of our material environment. Think about how single-sex dormitories and locker rooms presuppose that only heterosexual sex and desire exist. Or how the design of most homes builds in support for standard scripts about where we are supposed to have sex and in what position (very few homes have sex swings in the kitchen). Changing our cultural scripts is hard. But that doesn't mean that we can't actively and thoughtfully work together on slowly building new scripts that are specifically designed to enhance sexual pleasure and agency. For example, philosopher Tom Dougherty, in their essay "Social Scripts and Sexual Agency," points out that normalizing the establishment of safe words would give people a conventional, mutually understood script for ending a sexual encounter, just as handshaking scripts give us a shared conventional way to greet people respectfully. Likewise, social scripts that make it a standard part of polite foreplay to ask someone what gives them pleasure and what they dislike are also agency-enhancing; this practice is standard in kink contexts but not yet mainstream.

Agency is not the same as independence. I can act with agency even if I depend on the help or support of others to do so; for example, I may express my agency by asking you to let me sit on your shoulders so that I can see a concert over a crowd. In disability communities and disability studies scholarship, it has been fruitful to distinguish between *independence*, which is the ability to do things all on one's own, and *self-determination*, which a matter of driving one's own narrative and realizing one's own desires and values through one's actions. Early disability activism focused mostly on independence, but many advocates and scholars have pointed out that *no one* is truly independent. We all depend on material, institutional, social, and cultural support in order to act, from roads and trains to get us from one place to another, to grocery stores that provide us with food, to parents and friends and doctors who care for us when we are in need.

Self-determination does not require independence. We can be dependent but still self-determining if we are in a social ecology that supports us in shaping our own life and acting on our desires. When I pay for my child to go to the university of their own choosing, to study whatever they like, I am helping them be self-determining, even though they are dependent upon me. Likewise, sexual agency requires self-determination, but it does not require sexual independence. Our agency will always be dependent on the scripts, material possibilities, institutions, laws, relationships, and communities in which we are embedded.

Some groups of people systematically have less sexual agency than others, and accordingly, less access to sexual pleasure, fulfillment, and self-determination. For example, disabled people are widely desexualized by our culture and treated as inappropriate sexual partners. This narrows their range of potential partners. They also may face physical barriers to some sexual activities. Because they are often stuck in unequal power relations with other more privileged people, it is easier for them to be sexually abused or manipulated. Materially, many spaces designed for disabled people don't make room for sexual privacy or activity; transportation options may not make room for guests, which means that disabled people often cannot travel with their companion to go on a date, and institutions and rehabilitation centers may not provide private spaces. All these barriers require social solutions. We can build disability-accessible spaces that make room for intimacy and privacy; develop sex education curricula that explore options for disabled sexual pleasure; design sex toys specifically for disabled people; and work on introducing images of disabled erotic play and joy into the culture, for instance.

Pleasurable, consensual, self-expressive sex is a key part of a flourishing life for most people. We should think about how to make sexual agency *accessible* to as wide a range of people as possible, and this usually means enabling them to have good sex, not just to effectively avoid unwanted sex. In the twenty-first century, we are accustomed to thinking of access as a dimension of disability justice. I want to expand the notion of accessibility and think about how we can build a world in which sexual agency and good sex are as widely accessible as possible to all kinds of people, in full recognition of our imperfection, vulnerability, finitude, and dependencies. Our communal goal should be to create scaffolding for agency. We want to live in a world that builds up our agency, protects it, and holds it in place.

CHAPTER 4

Imperfect Autonomy

✖   ✖   ✖   ✖   ✖   ✖   ✖

IN 2015, HENRY RAYHONS WAS arrested for purportedly having sex with his wife, seventy-eight-year-old Donna Lou Rayhons, in her long-term care home. Her doctors had declared her incapable of consensual sex because of her dementia. She had little speaking ability left and could not remember her daughters' names or how to complete many simple daily tasks, but she always manifested pleasure and affection when her husband showed up. By everyone's report, they had a loving relationship with a long history and no signs of abuse. We cannot tell, from the details we get in this story, whether Henry respected and protected Donna's agency that day. What more would we need to know in order to decide?

Every day, millions of people get a little bit drunk or stoned before they have sex. Maybe you've done this on purpose now and again, to relax and to help you feel more social and less inhibited. I know I have. Did you feel safe? Did the two glasses of wine or the joint help you do what you wanted to do, or did they cloud your judgment? How might you tell?

54   SEX BEYOND "YES"

When we have sex, our autonomy is often imperfect. We have sex when we are fuzzy-headed, impaired, caught up in power relations, and aren't really sure what we are doing or what we want. People sleep with their supervisors, even though their supervisors could mess up their careers if things go badly. Teens have sex even in states and countries with abysmal sex education. Wives have begrudging sex when they feel they are not supposed to turn their husbands down.

Our autonomy can be less than perfect for internal reasons—if we are drunk, or have dementia or an intellectual disability, for instance. Or it can be compromised for external reasons—for example, if we are at the mercy of someone with power over us. Sometimes, our autonomy is so compromised that we lose the capacity for consensual sex. People who are blackout drunk, or who are threatened with being fired or fear violent abuse if they turn down sex, cannot have consensual sex. But we often have quite lovely sex despite imperfect autonomy. We get a little tipsy with our partner and go at it, or we meet someone at a club while on ecstasy and have a delightful time with them in a back room. Many people have fulfilling sexual relationships or even happy and healthy marriages with someone who has more money and social power than they do. These are much trickier cases.

A lot of public messaging about sex relies on a myth of an ideal autonomous self. According to this standard line, if someone is not completely able to know and rationally choose exactly what they want, then they cannot have consensual sex. But it virtually never happens that these conditions are met. The idea that we walk around making fully rational, self-reflective choices, free of any pressure and with complete information, is an unreachable and unhelpful fantasy. In reality, none of us can ever fully extract ourselves from unbalanced power relationships; our self-understanding is imperfect; our information is partial and usually distorted by ideology (especially when it comes to sex); our cognitive capacities are finite. And frankly, many of us find sex after a few drinks or tokes more relaxing and fun. If we were to insist on perfect autonomy as a condition for consent, then basically consensual sex would be impossible, and sex would either never happen or all of it would be rape.

Agency need not always involve independent control or conscious decision-making. If I am bouncing around happily to music, this may express my agency even if I am barely aware I am doing it and did not intentionally choose to do it. It is still self-determining action on my part, which expresses my desires and capacities to act, and is not manipulated. *Autonomy*, in contrast, is the capacity to make informed, conscious, independent, rational choices based on a clear understanding of one's preferences. Feminist legal scholar Deborah Tuerkheimer argues that we should focus on sexual agency, not sexual autonomy, because the language of autonomy suggests that we can be sovereign over ourselves, free of all social influences, and choose our sexual activities in a pure act of will. But none of us are such completely free and self-creating selves.

In light of the fact that our autonomy is almost always imperfect, we need to figure out at least two things. First, at what point is someone's autonomy so compromised that consensual sex is impossible? Second, how can we build social and interpersonal scaffolding that enables someone with imperfect autonomy—which is almost all of us, almost all of the time—to have consensual, even good, sex? The discussion I am undertaking here is a perilous one. Someone with little or no autonomy cannot have consensual sex, no matter how good the scaffolding. By emphasizing that we don't need perfect autonomy when we have sex, I am not legitimizing exploitative, unethical sex with people who cannot protect themselves. We don't need perfect autonomy to have

56   SEX BEYOND "YES"

ethical sex, but we do need at least minimal autonomy. But how much autonomy is enough? What is the minimum bar?

Bioethicist Agnieszka Jaworska proposes an understanding of "minimal autonomy" that she designed for the domain of medical decision-making, but I think it works well for sex too. Based on her proposal, I suggest that a *minimum* requirement for someone being autonomous enough to have consensual sex is (1) they can make a choice that is not directly manipulated, coerced, or extracted by someone else; (2) their own motivations are the source of their choice; and (3) they have enough capacity for reason and self-reflection that they can recognize reasons for and against what they are choosing to do—they are not simply acting on impulse. Someone who fails this third criterion cannot protect their own agency, but they also cannot protect the agency of their partner. Someone incapable of recognizing and respecting that their partner may have different desires from theirs should under no circumstances have sex.

Meeting this minimum standard is not enough to ensure agency or consensuality. For example, someone who grows up in an isolated cult and is raised to believe that they will go to hell if they don't have sex with its leader cannot really exercise agency in deciding whether to have sex with that leader—even if they are capable of understanding reasons, making decisions, and so forth. But the standard of minimal autonomy is necessary as a baseline. Someone who is so high on drugs that they are barely conscious, or hypnotized, or too intellectually compromised to be able to reason or reflect at all, cannot exercise sexual agency. On the other hand, a person who is mildly drunk, or who has moderate cognitive disabilities or a fluctuating memory, could meet all the conditions for minimal autonomy; at that point, the question is whether they have the scaffolding they need in order to exercise their agency. In the domain of medicine, health care providers and bioethicists know that people's ability to exercise agency and give consent depends on context. Someone with reduced cognitive capacities may well be unable to make well-considered medical choices in a disorienting, isolated hospital setting, but may be competent if they are at home with loved ones to talk to. Likewise, sexual agency and the capacity to have consensual sex are often fluctuating and context-dependent.

In thinking about internally compromised autonomy, I will start with drunken sex, because it is so common. Plenty of social messaging insists that drinking and consent are simply incompatible. "When drugs and alcohol are involved, clear consent cannot be obtained. An intoxicated person cannot give consent," warns one typical university website. The United States Military instructs recruits that drinking alcohol and consent are incompatible. But tipsy sex often happens after some drinks with dinner or after happy hour at the local pub. The idea that *all* such sex is nonconsensual is implausible. It's also just an unrealistic standard: We will never finger-wag drunken sex out of existence.

Researcher Trevor Goodyear and his colleagues recently studied how young men of various sexual orientations understood the intersection of alcohol and sex in their lives. These men talked a lot about worrying about whether they or their partners were too drunk to fuck, and about how alcohol could be weaponized as a way of "winning" sex from a reluctant partner. But interestingly, they also talked about how they used alcohol to build rather than undermine the scaffolding of sexual agency. Especially with prospective new partners, they said that having a drink or two created space and time to get to know someone and establish a connection with them. Many of them used alcohol to feel relaxed and social enough to be able to flirt and make a move. It

58   SEX BEYOND "YES"

let them work up to sex more slowly, feeling out whether it would be a good match and how the night should go. I have been with my partner for over a decade, but even now, we often have a drink together to create a social transition between the business of our day and sex. Of course, alcohol isn't essential to any of this, but we should recognize the positive role it can play in scaffolding good sex.

Whether drunken consensual sex is possible depends not only on how drunk everyone is, but on whether the specific circumstances, relationships, and negotiations support their agency. The mild fuzziness and lowered inhibitions that can come with a couple of drinks or tokes do not necessarily undermine our sexual agency. But finding ourselves unable to drive home if we need to can undercut our agency because it can strand us without a safe exit. Being tipsy might be enough to make real agency impossible in a disorienting new setting, but it might not challenge agency at all when one is at home with a trusted partner.

How do you know if you or your partner is too drunk to fuck? Imagine that you meet someone at a party after you've both had a few drinks, and you start fooling around. Giggling, you find a bedroom and start to undress. As you are about to go down on them, you ask, "Is this okay?" and your partner says "Yes!" and you end up wordlessly having oral sex. The next day, you feel unsettled. Was that "Yes!" actual consent? Did your partner really understand what they were agreeing to? How can you tell? All you have to go on was this one word, "yes." It's great that they apparently gave affirmative consent, but how drunk were they when they said it? Would they have felt comfortable saying no? What were they thinking and feeling when they said that word? The word "yes" is doing some heavy lifting as a measure of consent here. (Of course, if someone is too drunk to say "yes" at all, they are obviously too drunk to have consensual sex.)

Let's imagine the scenario somewhat differently. You meet someone at a party after a few drinks and start fooling around. In a flirtatious voice, you say to them, "Honestly, you're so hot. Can we do more? What would you like to do?" Your new friend responds, giggling, "I'm on my period, but you know, I have several other holes!" After some more banter, you have oral sex. As you go, you ask things like, "Are you comfortable? Would you like me to change anything?" Your partner assures you as you go that they are still having fun, but asks you to play with their breasts, which you do. When it comes to what feels like your turn, you say, "You know, I am really in a giving mood today. Would it be okay if we just stopped here?" Your partner agrees and thanks you. Now imagine that it's the next morning, and you are doing a check-in with yourself to make sure that you are comfortable with how things went. This time, it's quite hard to imagine how this kind of extended discussion was actually just an outgrowth of impulsive incompetence or discomfort. If we were in the habit of having more extended sexual negotiations, talking about our likes, limits, and desires, and checking in with one another as we went, the worry that we could mistakenly look competent to ourselves or someone else would be less plausible because we would have put our competence and our ability to make thoughtful decisions on display during communication. Negotiations and check-ins can be an enormous help in scaffolding drunk sex and ensuring that it expresses agency. And if we or our partner can't make it coherently through any such conversation, well, there's our answer right there, and consensual sex is out of the question.

Thinking about the sexual agency of people with moderate dementia is particularly challenging and important. Sex later in life is correlated with lower rates of depression, more self-care, and higher markers of general well-being. Yet a third of us who make it to old age

60   SEX BEYOND "YES"

will eventually have some form of dementia. Dementia is associated with an increase in libido in 14 percent of people, and with a decrease in almost none of them. We know that people with dementia typically crave and take pleasure from touch, including sexual touch, often long after they have lost other desires and pleasures. Indeed, a significant number of people with dementia become sexually aggressive and demanding. While experiencing sexual desire and benefiting from sex do not add up to consensuality or agency, this is powerful evidence that we should enable people with dementia to have consensual sex, if possible.

Long-term care homes for older people, including people with dementia, are often places where standard intimate connections have been severed or lost and touch is highly regulated. Many residents come to them following the death of a longtime partner. When residents with dementia try to start sexual relationships with one another, these are typically discouraged. These facilities generally treat sexual activity among residents as a legal risk and probably nonconsensual, and hence best prevented. There are a handful of explicitly sex-positive facilities, but they are rare and controversial. Staff at long-term care facilities generally receive little or no training in supporting residents' sex lives and do not think the opportunity to remain sexually active is important for residents. Residents usually face physical and spatial barriers to intimacy, including doors that can't be locked and little or no access to private spaces. Meanwhile, our cultural norm of treating older people as generally asexual, and indeed treating the entire topic of sex among the older people as disgusting and off-limits, contributes to an environment in which older people have few resources for understanding their own sexual desires or accessing good information about sex.

In an antagonistic environment of this sort, where the only way to have sex is furtively, under threat of being found out and reprimanded, it is impossible to get the kind of social support that would make sex safe for someone with fluctuating or marginal capacities. Stress enhances cognitive deficits, so residents who are sneaking around and breaking rules are also not likely to be at their most competent. There may well be no one trustworthy to go to with questions or concerns if they have any. If they are already hiding their sexual activities, it may be harder for them to exit a sexual situation or relationship if they want to, especially if they also have mobility challenges. In other words, the entire environment is often hostile to its residents' sexual agency and need for sexual intimacy. In contrast, a culture that treats sexual intimacy as valuable and normal among older people would foster a sex-positive environment that provides privacy, support, sexual health care, and regular sexual counseling. These would scaffold the agency of people with imperfect autonomy due to dementia.

Henry Rayhons was acquitted of all charges, and we cannot be sure that he had sex with his wife that day or what the circumstances were if so. If they did have sex, I hope that he was ready to stop immediately if his wife showed any sign of fear, discomfort, or disengagement, and that he waited for her more lucid and communicative moments before initiating sex. Elder abuse is rampant, and the husband of a person with dementia may just have his way with her, rather than responsively and responsibly supporting her agency. But given what we know about the general desire for sexual intimacy among people with dementia and its connection to their well-being, we should not presume that their sex was nonconsensual. It is completely possible that someone may genuinely want a sexual encounter, and that that encounter may be a good expression of who they are, their values, and the kind of thing they enjoy, even if their autonomy is compromised. A good partner can use sensitive and responsive communication and attention, a rich understanding of their partner's past, and clearly established exit conditions to help give them the stability and safety they need to have good consensual sex. Conversely, someone who demeans, dehumanizes, or humiliates their partner, or insults their intelligence or self-esteem, chips away at their ability to act with agency, undermining their self-trust and their sense that their own desires are worth expressing and protecting.

An important ethical task we owe one another is what I call *holding one another in agency*. I base this idea on feminist philosopher Hilde Lindemann's notion of "holding in personhood." Lindemann shows that many of the roles and identities that are most central to our sense of self and our integrity require social support. As our ability to hold onto our sense of self and to act in line with our values and commitments wavers and becomes vulnerable—through illness, addiction, dementia, or trauma, perhaps—others need to step up and take over more of the labor of holding us in personhood. For example, we can support someone's compromised ability to be themselves by picking out a record for them that accords with their tastes and adds to their collection; caring for and giving them updates about a beloved pet; giving them a manicure or a haircut; or calling them by their professional title. These are small acts of self-care and self-maintenance that others can do for us when we are unable to maintain our identity by ourselves.

Just as we can hold someone in personhood, we can also hold them in agency. That is, just as I can help someone to be themselves, I can also help someone express themselves in action, especially when it is hard for them to do this on their own. A partner can protect their vulnerable loved one's agency by being a good, skilled, and caring interpreter of their expressions of pleasure, pain, desire, embarrassment, comfort, fear, and the like. When it comes to an intimate encounter, holding someone in their agency requires being competently responsive to their gestures and their nascent expressions, while also respecting and understanding who they are, what they value, and so forth. Typically, a long-term, caring partner will be best positioned to detect subtle signs of desire, discomfort, agitation, and pleasure in someone whose ability to communicate and remember are compromised. A person with compromised capacities may well be able to have consensual sex with one partner, who holds them in agency well, while being incapable of having consensual sex with a different partner who is less able or willing to scaffold their agency.

Sexual exploration is often an important part of sexual flourishing. But partners of people with imperfect autonomy should not exploit an impulse that does not cohere with that person's usual values and sense of self. When people are in a good position to have strong autonomy, free from any special vulnerabilities, they can freely choose to try out sexual activities and scenarios that are substantially out of step with their prior experiences and desires. However, when someone's autonomy is compromised, it is not the right time for experimenting with pushing new boundaries or radical new possibilities. There is an important difference between a normally shy and sexually reserved person becoming more outgoing and experimental after a few drinks, which may be harmless and freeing, and someone wanting things when cognitively impaired that radically break with their own values and usual sense of self.

So far, we've been discussing internal compromises of autonomy, but our autonomy can also be compromised by our external situation, even if we are fully cognitively capable of independent, reflective, informed choice. Most obviously, if someone is directly forced or coerced into doing something, for example by being threatened with violence or blackmail, then their choice to do it is not autonomous. But more interesting cases involve subtler power differentials. Sex partners can have unequal power because of differences between their ages, abilities, institutional roles (supervisor and employee, teacher and student), social standing, immigration status, race, or finances. One partner may have more power because they have better family support and a stronger friend network, while the other partner is more isolated and socially dependent on the relationship. Or one partner may be ridiculously attractive and extroverted and have a much easier time finding sexual partners.

On the one hand, power differentials can compromise the autonomy of a less powerful partner whose sexual choices may not be fully extricable from other social pressures (financial dependence, concerns about their career, and so forth). On the other hand, once we start listing possible sources of power inequality, it quickly becomes clear that we are all tightly enmeshed in dense, inescapable, endlessly complex webs of power relationships. The sources of possible power differences between partners are virtually unending. The idea of a *pure* relationship between partners who are *exact equals* is mythological. Likewise, the idea that any power differential precludes consensual sex is unrealistic.

In the medical domain, we all know that doctors and their patients don't have symmetrical power. Doctors have institutional and social authority, and the ability to gravely harm or help their patients. Patients regularly go to doctors for help when they are especially vulnerable and unable to do things they normally can do. Even patients who are quite powerful in everyday contexts often feel disempowered in a medical setting. And yet no one thinks that power imbalances and vulnerabilities in the medical domain make legitimate consent to health care impossible. We understand that although patient autonomy is imperfect, we should not give up on it. Instead, we should find ways to bolster and protect patients' agency despite nonideal conditions. In order to support patients' imperfect autonomy, we design patient decision tools and institutional checks and balances, and we think about where, with whom, and when patients should make decisions, with the help of what kinds of conversations.

We should take a similar approach to thinking about sexual agency within power imbalances. People at a power disadvantage should not be assumed to be incapable of consensual sex. Consensual, wanted sex is possible even when there are pressures and inequalities that constrain our options, impose unfortunate risks on us, and make our choices less than fully autonomous. Different kinds of sexual relationships require different levels of scaffolding and can tolerate different kinds of imperfections. A one-night stand at a sex club can be unproblematically consensual even if one partner is much wealthier or older or whatever; such differences are unlikely to poison the dynamic of a quick, hot hookup. In contrast, a long-term relationship may be deeply structured by such power differences in troubling ways.

When a couple has a power differential, ideally mechanisms should be in place to ensure the more powerful partner doesn't abuse their power. For example, in academic settings, if a professor and a graduate student or a full professor and an untenured junior professor start a relationship, usually university policies are in place that keep the more powerful partner from having direct say over the less powerful partner's grades, tenure case, and so forth. I don't think such policies are sufficient to erase worries about those relationships, but they are an example of the kind of social scaffolding I have in mind, and they do help.

Surely the most pervasive example of sex across power differences

66   SEX BEYOND "YES"

is heterosexual sex under patriarchy. There is a standing default power differential between men and women, although this is complicated by other kinds of intersecting power differentials such as those based on differences in race or class. There are all sorts of reasons to think that women's autonomy—and especially their sexual autonomy—is substantially diminished under patriarchy, particularly but not only in their interactions with heterosexual men. Women under patriarchy are often objectified, degraded, and dehumanized in ways that make recognition of and respect for their agency difficult. Philosopher and feminist social critic Kate Manne has argued influentially that patriarchy is structured by norms that demand that women serve men's needs, and that sexuality is a central arena in which such servitude is demanded. Growing up as a woman under patriarchy involves developing attitudes and habits that are tangled deep within pervasive expectations that women be passive rather than assertive, especially when it comes to sex, and quiet about their own sexual desires and preferences. This can diminish women's ability to effectively refuse sex with men. Women who try to refuse sex with men often face verbal abuse or worse. Patriarchy also undermines women's credibility when they try to report or discuss rape and sexual assault. Patriarchy thus works along multiple axes to curtail women's sexual autonomy.

If only perfect equals could have consensual sex, then women could never have consensual heterosexual sex under patriarchy. In effect, all heterosexual sex would be rape. Such a view would make the notion of rape nearly useless and unprosecutable. It is also unacceptably insulting and paternalistic to tell straight and bisexual women that none of the sex they are having with men, including the sex they actively seek out, is consensual. For all the many problems and pitfalls surrounding heterosexual sex, there's plenty of good, happy, wanted, fulfilling heterosexual sex; it's not useful or illuminating to say that all such sex is rape even when it is welcomed and delightful. Indeed, it makes a mockery of the serious wrong of rape to do so. This means that we need to understand how legitimately consensual heterosexual sex under patriarchy is possible for women.

Patriarchy almost by definition disempowers women. But we should not be skeptical of the possibility of consensual straight sex. Instead, we should work to create social scaffolding that makes straight sex as pleasurable and empowered as possible for women as well as men under patriarchy. This can include making sure that women are given at least some exposure to feminist thought and critiques of misogyny and patriarchy so that they can be self-reflective about their choices and the norms they are embedded in. It includes helping women discover what gives them sexual pleasure, and not just how to say "no" to men effectively. It also includes ensuring access to contraception and abortion; social resources and safe spaces for people who are trying to leave abusive or coercive relationships; social and legal accountability for men who sexually violate women; a justice system and a culture that acknowledge that sexual violation is common and not the fault of the victim; strong communities of women who can share their experiences and stabilize and recognize one another's sense of reality; and a culture that does not shame women who want and enjoy sex with men.

However we scaffold sex across gendered power differentials, it is not just going to be a matter of individual men kindly choosing not to avail themselves of the power and privileges given to them by patriarchy. We need social scaffolding and structural change, not just "nice guys" who voluntarily refrain from abusing women. Many of the forces that reduce women's sexual autonomy are structural, not individual. If a man decides that he will personally take "no" for an answer with-

68   SEX BEYOND "YES"

out responding abusively, or that he will be attentive and responsive to a woman's expressed desires and discomforts, this is not enough to ensure his partner's agency. If someone has the power to harm someone else or to undercut their agency, it is nice for them to promise not to use this power, but that doesn't make the power go away. Power is real, and the possibility of its exercise shapes our choices. In *The Joy of Consent*, Manon Garcia recognizes that sexual negotiation is virtually never between perfect equals. She stresses that it is the job of the more powerful partner to "create conditions for equality" and "make sure the person who has less power can express themselves without fear." I agree, but, short of concretely divesting themselves of their power (which is often not possible and usually not practical), there is only so much that a more powerful partner can do to create these conditions. As kinky sex educator Icarus put it to me in an interview, "There is no such thing as a negotiation so good that its outside—society and power differentials—no longer exists." We need institutional and community scaffolding that materially protects less-powerful partners from being exploited or trapped. For example, we can set up mechanisms and services that help people leave relationships in which they have less power, and this can help make consensual sexual relationships possible across power differentials.

Some unequal relationships are asymmetrical enough, with enough potential for harm and manipulation, that there is just no possibility of consensual sex, regardless of scaffolding. To give an extreme example, we all agree that parent-child sex could never possibly be consensual and is always repugnant (even if the child appears to agree to the relationship). As obvious as this may seem, it's worth thinking about why exactly this is. First, the relationships of authority and hierarchy within families are just too entrenched. Families have deeply embedded and complex power arrangements. Children are fundamentally at the mercy of their parents and usually grow up seeing them as authority figures who there are costs to disobeying. Second, incest is so stigmatized that a victim of incest would have no community support; they would be completely isolated in that relationship. And finally, our society is set up in such a way that it is extremely hard to truly exit from one's family. People manage it, but at high cost, and many people who want to extricate themselves fail. This is a type of relationship that can never be made consensual through negotiations or scaffolding.

The case of philosophy professor Anna Stubblefield, who was imprisoned for rape in 2015, provides a real-life example of a sexual relationship in which consensuality was impossible. Stubblefield—who, ironically, wrote about disability ethics—was conducting research on and providing professional support to a young black man, D.J. D.J. has cerebral palsy, and it is unclear to what extent he also has intellectual disabilities. He is nonverbal, although Stubblefield claimed he could talk to her through facilitated communication. Facilitated communication is a scientifically contested practice in which nonverbal people supposedly type with someone helping to guide their hands. Stubblefield revealed to D.J.'s family that she and he were having a sexual relationship, which she claimed was a consensual love relationship.

There were massive power differences between Stubblefield and D.J. along multiple dimensions. She was his therapist and mentor; she enjoyed racial, educational, social, and economic privileges that he did not; and, most obviously, he depended on her to communicate in language, assuming that he could do so at all, which is unclear. What is most striking to me about the case is how impossible it was for D.J. to meaningfully refuse sex with Stubblefield, exit from his relationship with her, or seek any kind of social support or resources. He had mobility challenges that made him physically unable to resist sexual advances or to leave of his own accord. He could *only* communicate with Stubblefield, so he literally could not turn to others to discuss or question his relationship or ask for help or information, unmediated by her. And during actual sex, he would have been unable to talk even with her—presuming that they were using their hands at the time for activities other than assisted typing—which means he could not tell her to stop or ask her to adjust. Her power over him was total and unmitigable. For all these reasons, consensual sex between them was an impossibility.

There are people who defended Stubblefield. Some claimed that the charges against her were ableist, as they implied that profoundly disabled people were unworthy of sex or love. Certainly, D.J. is deserving of love and pleasure, and I don't doubt that Stubblefield felt love for him, but that does not mean he could have consensual sex with her. There are many ways of showing someone love and even giving them physical pleasure without having sex with them. Two famous philosophers, Peter Singer and Jeff McMahan, published a *New York Times* opinion piece in 2017 claiming that Anna Stubblefield was the "real victim," because she loved D.J. and hence she could not count as raping him. "This is the action not of a sexual predator but of an honest and honorable woman in love. . . . This ought to have been a mitigating, if not wholly exculpating, consideration in the sentencing," they write. But of course many sexual predators "love" their victims. People "in love" sometimes stalk, rape, and even murder the objects of their love. Love is zero excuse for any kind of abuse or sexual violation. Rapists are people who have nonconsensual sex with others. Their own mental attitudes toward and emotions about their victims are no measure whatsoever of whether they committed rape. Singer and McMahan also claimed that D.J. benefited from the relationship because he probably found the sex pleasurable (presumably because he is a man, and men supposedly always enjoy sex?). But D.J.'s hypothesized pleasure is not the issue; his total subjugation to Stubblefield is. Many rape victims are ashamed of their experiences of physiological pleasure reactions during sex. But their internal sensations are not the measure of whether they were raped.

As a society, we are generally uncomfortable with the idea of sex with imperfect autonomy. When someone has compromised capacities, we generally think of sex as dangerous and shameful for them. When someone has reduced power within a sexual relationship, we either simply disapprove of that relationship, or we tell sugarcoated myths that deny that the power differential exists: misogynist myths of seductively controlling women; or racist myths of over-sexed people of color; or romantic myths of love that is somehow so magical that it erases social power differentials. We often hear that people who do not have perfect autonomy—intoxicated people, teenagers, people with cognitive disabilities, oppressed people—"cannot give consent." Often, although not always, such people have all the capacities they need in order to have consensual sex and express their agency. They have the capacity to reflect on their desires and preferences, respond to reasons, make choices, and communicate those choices. The problem is that they may not be in circumstances or relationships that support those capacities. I suggest that we focus less on measuring whether people's capacities are intact and more on creating the conditions for agency. We should develop, curate, and explore examples of well-scaffolded consensual sex under imperfect conditions. We should be as well versed in how to make good sex possible in nonideal real-world conditions as we are in how sex can go awry.

CHAPTER 5

Ambivalence and Agency

✖　　　✖　　　✖　　　✖　　　✖　　　✖　　　✖

love hiking, and I have great endurance, but I am afraid of heights and prone to vertigo. You invite me on a gorgeous-looking hike. I know that it might be too much for me, but I also know that if I manage it, I will be super proud of myself and I will have a fantastic time. But I just can't tell in advance if it's going to be exhilarating, terrifying, or unmanageable.

I am an amateur boxer. I love fighting, but each time I am about to get in the ring, I doubt my choice. I can't predict what will happen in advance. I can be pretty sure that some moments of the fight are going to be painful and discouraging—it's not like I will get through the whole event without being punched! And fighting is risky; the whole thing might end with injury, humiliation, or both. But when fighting goes well, it is the most thrilling thing that I experience in my life.

My partner wants to practice bondage with me. I know that letting them tie me up and suspend me would give them great pleasure, and the idea does interest me and turn me on a bit. But I have never experienced it, and I am not sure if I might feel panicky, or uncomfortable, or maybe even just silly once we do it. Honestly, I am not sure how I feel about it.

Each of these three scenarios is grounded in experiences from my life. In each, I feel ambivalent about whether I want to do something together with someone else, both in the sense that I am unsure whether I want to do the thing, and also in the sense that I am unsure what the experience of doing it would be like; I don't know if it will be exhilarating, frightening, painful, embarrassing, pride-inducing, or some mix of these. In each case, I have to decide whether to participate in a joint activity with someone else that leaves me vulnerable to various kinds of physical and emotional harm, while at the same time giving me the possibility of joy, pleasure, and satisfaction.

When I am feeling unsure whether to go on the hike, what might my concerns be? I don't really know how scary or difficult the hike will be, or how I will react to the challenge. But I also may be worried that I will disappoint or anger you if I bail on the hike in the middle, or that you will try to pressure me into continuing. I might very well be concerned that bailing or showing fear will be embarrassing. I might also worry that I won't be able to turn around if I want to because it may be too hard to get back down.

In the case of the boxing match, my concerns may be overlapping, but also distinct. I might worry that I am biting off more than I can chew—I could be injured or overwhelmed during the fight. Honestly, when I am getting ready for a fight, I am also always worried that I will be mocked or embarrassed if I can't make it through to the end. But I also worry about the referee calling the fight too soon; what if I accidentally look distressed or hurt or tired, and the referee ends the fight or gives me an eight-count when I still have plenty of fight left in me? I recognize that I can never know exactly what to expect from my opponent; it's not like I can ask in advance which blows they intend to throw. Nor can I insist that I be asked for verbal consent before each punch. That would entirely destroy the fun and the point of the match; the Antioch Policy decidedly does not work as a model of consent for combat sports!

Finally, what might my concerns be in the bondage and suspension case? I might not enjoy being tied up—it could be uncomfortable or claustrophobic or just not a turn-on; I might feel quite silly once we get going. I might worry about the possibility of injury. I might be concerned that if I start to panic, it's going to be a difficult and lengthy process to untie me. I might worry about whether I will be able to speak up and express my needs if I want to readjust; if I express any displeasure or try to control what is happening, will it wreck the mood? As in the hiking case, I might well also worry that my partner will be disappointed, angry, or frustrated if I want to stop.

Some of these concerns, such as injury and physical discomfort, are specific to physically risky or edgy activities, but many of the others apply to any joint activity in which I am not sure what it will be like: whether I will like it, how my body or emotions will respond, or how my partner will respond if I want or need to stop or redirect the activity. Any kind of sexual terrain can generate these sorts of concerns and this kind of ambivalence. Even if nothing kinky is going on, I might be ambivalent about having sex with a new partner; or having sex in a new environment; or having sex for the first time.

We cannot always clearly and univocally state that yes, we want to do some sexual activity, or no, we do not, because we are often legitimately unsure—unsure what we want, and unsure what we will experience if we decide to begin. Feminist sexuality scholar Katherine Angel, in her book *Tomorrow Sex Will Be Good Again*, opens with the fact that we often don't know what we want when it comes to sex; we are pulled in different directions and can't always know what will give us pleasure in advance. This kind of ambivalence and vulnerability is clearly not specific to sex, but sex is a primary example of a domain where it comes up. Sexual ambivalence is not a bad thing in and of itself. When we are interested in pushing our own boundaries and questioning dominant assumptions about what we should be doing, it stands to reason that we will often find ourselves unsure of what exactly we want or what it would be like to try something.

Angel describes sexual ambivalence as a distinctive issue for women, who, she thinks, are not trained to be certain of their desires. But men and nonbinary people are perfectly capable of sexual ambivalence as well. I think Angel's focus on women is based on the widespread but troubling assumption that men basically always want sex, and hence always know what they want, while ambivalence is women's domain. If anything, though, men might be especially bad at understanding and articulating their own sexual desires, precisely because they are trained up on the idea that they are supposed to just want to put their dick in whatever they can, whenever they can. We do not give men a lot of room or tools for sexual subtlety or self-reflection in our culture!

If you feel genuinely ambivalent, you cannot simply make and communicate an informed choice about what you want to do. In the situations I described earlier, my desires were legitimately unclear, unsettled, and indeterminate, and some crucial information about how the future would go was unknowable to me. I could not predict in advance whether I would feel vertigo, or how the fight would unfold, or how I would respond to being tied up. Ambivalence makes our autonomy imperfect, but perfect autonomy is not a realistic or helpful ideal.

76   SEX BEYOND "YES"

Many discussions of sexual agency insist that only fully informed, completely confident consent counts as consent at all. But full information and certainty of pleasure are just what we cannot have in these ambivalent situations.

Sometimes, consent is defined merely as not saying "no." Clearly, that kind of consent is insufficient for protecting our agency in these sorts of cases. If I am not sure whether I want to do something, my failure to say "no" does not constitute a "yes." If you challenge me to a boxing match, and I do not say "no," that doesn't mean you get to punch me in the face! But affirmative consent is also not a sufficient standard in this situation. First, what's interesting to think about here is how we can get from ambivalence to a "yes" or a "no" in a way that preserves and buttresses our agency. Second, if I do affirmatively consent while feeling ambivalent, that doesn't mean my ambivalence has been resolved or adequately managed. I may say "yes" while still being unsure what I am consenting to, and I may still worry about ending up humiliated, hurt, in conflict with my partner, unable to exit the situation, and so forth. In other words, although it is certainly true that if your partner is ambivalent about an activity, it is important to wait for a clear "yes" from them before proceeding, the affirmative consent standard doesn't tell us anything interesting about how to scaffold agency under these sorts of murky conditions.

Importantly, *enthusiastic consent* is exactly the wrong standard in ambivalent situations. I am not enthusiastic or full-throated in my desire to participate in the hike, the fight, or the bondage; that's the whole point. If we require enthusiastic consent for all sexual activities, then we rule out doing anything that we feel ambivalent about. But we do not demand enthusiasm as a precondition for action in other domains of life. Think how silly it would be to claim that you only count as proofreading your essay or washing the dishes consensually so long as you do so with enthusiasm; or that you have to be enthusiastic about watching a television show with your partner on a boring Wednesday evening when you're both exhausted and out of ideas for what else to do; or that you have to be super into having that wart of yours sliced off in order to consent to medical treatment. I may consent to going on a vacation with a high-maintenance friend even if I am worried it will turn out to be a mistake. We consensually do things that we are not enthusiastic about all the time! Why should sex be any different?

In many kink contexts, where consent is heavily discussed and theorized, people like to define consensual sex in terms of FRIES: Consent is supposed to be freely given, reversible, informed, enthusiastic, and specific. (Kinksters love their consent definitions, and this is only one model among several popular ones!) It is certainly true that consensuality requires that everyone must be participating freely, without manipulation or coercion. As for reversibility, I will have lots to say about that shortly. But the other three elements of FRIES don't seem to work in the kinds of murky, ambivalent contexts I've described. We just saw that enthusiasm is not a reasonable prerequisite for sex. And we also saw that we cannot always be fully informed, because we may try something new and be unable to know how it will go or how we will feel about it. Sometimes, as in the boxing case, we cannot be specific in advance about what we are agreeing to because surprise and imperfect control are built into the activity. As Katherine Angel puts it, traditional "consent culture" doesn't tell us how to cope with ambivalence. The idea that people should always clearly state their informed and enthusiastic desires is inadequate to contexts in which there is no full advance information to be had, and no clear desire to be stated.

The response to all this from someone who is a big FRIES fan may

78   SEX BEYOND "YES"

well be: "Well, if you're so unsure about doing something, just don't do it! Ambivalent agency isn't good, strong agency." This idea that if either you or your partner are unsure, then you just shouldn't proceed, is so common that "'I'm not sure' means no!" makes it onto multiple memes and infographics about consent, as does the idea that "Consent requires an enthusiastic 'yes.'" A recent queer music and sex festival in Germany sported signs that read, "Push your look, not your limits!"

But this restriction would deal far too serious a blow to our sexual agency and our opportunities for sexual pleasure and fulfillment. More generally, our lives would be much less self-determining, empowered, and fulfilling if we simply steered clear of ever pushing our limits or ever doing things about which we felt ambivalent. The freedom to push our boundaries, explore our limits, and figure out what we enjoy and can achieve expands our positive agency. We just have *fewer things we can do* if we believe that we can't do anything we are unsure about. And some of the things we feel ambivalent about we may well turn out to like, or even love. We may discover talents and capacities we never thought we had. Our possibilities for intense and varied forms of pleasure and fulfillment shoot up if we sometimes take a plunge even though we are uncertain.

Even apart from this broadening of our experiences, pushing ourselves and taking risks is inherently agency-expanding, not to mention exciting and satisfying. We often feel most empowered and perhaps even at our most self-determining when we are pressing on the edges of our comfort zone, rather than acting on our settled prior preferences. Taking a leap that pushes our boundaries isn't a diminished or partial form of agency. On the contrary, our ability to take such risks is often an especially intense flexing of our agency! Our world becomes narrow and restricted and our agency atrophies if we never push our limits.

This is true for life in general: for hiking and fighting, adventurous travel, becoming a parent, moving in with a partner, taking a challenging new job, and more. And it holds for sex as well. Our sex lives are much smaller, with less possibility for fulfillment and discovery, if we only do predictable things that we are already sure we will enjoy. We discover what we like and want by trying things out with the right kind of support, not just by being given the right to informed consent or refusal. This is why it is valuable to protect and scaffold people's ability to make risky choices in the face of ambivalence.

What can we do to help people make good-quality decisions about what to do when they are ambivalent? How can we help people safely and freely explore and push their boundaries; decide when it is *not* the right time to try something; and retain their agency in the midst of a potentially overwhelming or unpleasant activity?

Perhaps the most important way to scaffold ambivalent agency is by setting up easy and cost-free exit conditions. If I am considering trying something where I am not sure how it will go or whether I will like it, I probably care a great deal about whether I can *stop* or *leave* easily if I want or need to. I am more likely to push my own limits if I know I can retreat. Think about my three opening scenarios, and how many of my possible concerns were about what would happen if I wanted to stop. I may be worried about the physical possibility of stopping (Can I be untied quickly? Can I make it back down the mountain?); my partner's reaction to my trying to stop (Anger? Disappointment or hurt feelings? Mockery? Trying to convince me to continue?); the social response to my stopping (Losing cred? Teasing?); or my own personal feelings about stopping (Embarrassment? Disappointment in myself?). The traditional consent framework tends to focus on ensuring agency at the *start* of sex but in ambivalent scenarios, it is especially

80   SEX BEYOND "YES"

clear that agency depends at least as much on controlling one's ability to exit the situation.

In boxing and other combat sports, we build in rules that allow people to stop an activity unambiguously and immediately by giving a preordained sign that functions as a safe word: tapping out or not standing during an eight-count, for instance. Likewise, to support agency, exit conditions in ambivalent sexual situations should be unambiguous, accepted by everyone involved, physically easy to enact, and detached from any blame, recrimination, pressure, shaming, social punishment, or haggling. Safe words and other clear exit signals, even if we never use them, can enhance agency both by expanding the range of things we are willing to try in the first place, and by keeping us safe and empowering us during the activity.

My hiking scenario was based directly on an experience I had in Norway a few years ago. A friend who knows I enjoy physical activity was hosting me in her small town and suggested that we take a hike together on the outskirts of town. I was nervous about it because of my fear of heights, but I also wanted to see the beautiful landscape, get some exercise, and spend time with my friend. Almost as soon as we started hiking, I knew I was in trouble. The path was solid ice, angling down on one side toward a sheer drop. I immediately felt dizzy and unstable. I said to my friend, "Hmm, this is going to be challenging for me, I am not great with heights." She lightly agreed that the path was icy. As we walked, I felt increasingly panicky, and I tried to communicate to my friend that I wanted to turn around. "I'm really not sure I want to do this!" I said. She was taking time out of her day to do something with me she thought would be fun, so I did not want to be rude; I put my laments gently and indirectly. She, for her part, quite naturally took my pushback as reason to encourage me: "I do this walk all the time," she said. "People come here with their kids, and no one ever falls. You'll be fine!"

My friend's response made sense; in many contexts, such encouragement would be exactly the right response. "I am feeling unsure I want to continue" doesn't always mean "No," even though that's what I was trying to convey. It can just as easily mean, "Help me feel confident about continuing." Finally, I had to basically shout at her, "NO! I WANT TO GO BACK NOW!" Of course, she was gracious, and we turned around right away. But my direct "No!" came off as a confrontational social rupture, and she apologized profusely—both results that I wanted to avoid, as she had done nothing wrong.

Think about how much better this whole situation could have gone if I had said up front, "Hey, I want to try this, but just so you know, I am afraid of heights and prone to vertigo. If I call 'Red,' that means I definitely want to turn around right then. Thanks for taking me, I am excited to try this!" If we had scaffolded my exit options in this way, I could have saved myself a lot of anxiety and feelings of disempowerment; I could have avoided conflict and awkwardness with my friend; and I could have protected her feelings. In many social encounters, including sexual encounters, the more ambivalent we feel about trying something with someone else, especially when there is plenty of room for vulnerability and feelings of rejection, the more important it is to scaffold an easy exit.

Clear negotiation up front is important, but materially scaffolding our ability to exit also helps support our agency in the face of ambivalence and uncertainty. I might want to make sure that I have an easy way back down a mountain on a hike. Or that scissors are right on hand for releasing me quickly during a bondage scene. Or that before I go out with someone, I have an easy way to get home, or a friend to call who will come get me.

82   SEX BEYOND "YES"

Cultural and community scaffolding are important as well. For example, it is harder to exit an activity if I suspect that I will end up being socially punished for having participated in the first place. Some people are scared to seek help leaving abusive relationships for fear of being berated for having been in them to start with. People can be put off from trying kinky or edgy sex practices that interest them by their reasonable fear that if something goes wrong and they need help, they will be shamed and reprimanded, or worse, by hospital staff or police officers. (At one sex festival I attended, one of the participants injured her neck during a choking scene. Some people were worried the whole festival would be shut down if she was truthful with the hospital about what had happened.)

Imagine that you really want to try jumping off the high diving board, but you're unsure whether you can bring yourself to go through with it. If there is a crowd of people below who are going to mock you for walking to the edge and then turning around, or who will try to cajole and badger you into jumping once you get there, I suspect that you're much less likely to get onto the board in the first place than you would be if you were alone or with supportive friends. And if you do go up onto it, you're going to feel much more pressure to jump, and less able to make your own self-determining decision.

We currently have social scripts and cultural practices that shame folks for transitioning genders and then detransitioning later, accusing them of "faking" or holding them up as proof that trans identities are invalid. Similarly, we routinely shame folks for having a straight relationship after a queer one, accusing them of taking the easy way out (and my fellow queers are at least as guilty of doing this to people as straight people are). Such scripts and tropes discourage people from feeling safe enough to explore what gender identity and sexual relationships would make them happiest and most fulfilled by threatening them with social punishment for changing their mind.

We do not always want people to be able to change their minds and back out of choices at will without consequence. If I promise you that I will feed your dog while you are in the hospital, it should not be easy and cost free for me to abruptly say, "Actually, I am not feeling this, I'm not enjoying your dog, I've changed my mind." We would rightly expect some social penalties and accountability for that kind of behavior. If I become a parent, I cannot stop taking care of my child on a whim. If I run for mayor and am elected, my constituents should expect me to stick with the job unless I truly cannot, and they are right to blame me if I quit for my own convenience. All this is true even if I felt ambivalent from the start about feeding your dog, becoming a parent, or running for mayor. Yet when it comes to sex, we want people to be able to change their minds about participating at any moment, without penalty, no excuse necessary. How can we distinguish between the kinds of decisions that it is ethically appropriate to hold people accountable for sticking with and those where we want to make exit easy? At a minimum, when an activity involves intimate bodily vulnerabilities of the sort that might lay someone open to harm, and when this is not true for anyone else who depends on their activities, making it easy for them to exit the activity seems morally required.

Unsurprisingly, different people feel ambivalent about different things. Sometimes it is a good bet that your partner might feel ambivalent about something: physically risky sadomasochistic play, combat sports, paragliding. When you plan to deviate from familiar social scripts or from activities that people are typically comfortable with, you need to begin by assuming your partner is likely to feel ambivalence. This is your responsibility, and it is part of caring for your partner's well-being and agency. But people can also be unpredictably ambivalent about surprising things. No one who knows me casually would presume that I am afraid of heights. My long-term sweetie with whom I have had sex hundreds of times would have no reason to suspect, on a given night, that I am feeling ambivalent about cozy vanilla sex, but perhaps something upset or disoriented me that day and I am feeling especially off-kilter and vulnerable. In such cases, it is my responsibility to let my partner know that I am feeling ambivalent, and that extra layers of negotiation and scaffolding are needed. This is what I owe my partner and myself. No one can be expected to guess the many things that might make someone else have ambivalent feelings, and it's impracticable to negotiate and scaffold every single sexual encounter to death, just in case. As kink educators and performers Lief and Icarus put it, your partner's protection of your agency is your *right*, but communicating with them well in ways that enable them to protect you is your *responsibility*. This responsibility includes letting your partner know when you are feeling ambivalent in unpredictable ways.

When everyone is participating by choice, exit is easy, and communication is working well, sex can be consensual even when we enter it ambivalently. But we've seen that sexual agency requires more than just consensuality. We can express our agency despite our ambivalence when there are interpersonal, material, cultural, and community conditions in place that let us start, stop, and adjust when we want, without fear of bullying, recrimination, shame, pressure, or harm. There is no guarantee that when we enter sex ambivalently, we will have a good time or be glad we chose it. This is a risk we take when we decide to dive in. Yet risky choices have the potential to lead to great experiences. Pushing our limits can be fulfilling and exhilarating, as well as consensual and agency-enhancing.

Navigating consent and agency when we are feeling ambivalent or when our partner is feeling ambivalent is tricky and can sometimes require ninja-grade communication skills. Just making sure that your partner really said "yes" doesn't come close to protecting their agency. But at the same time—and this is a point that is particularly close to my heart—this doesn't mean that we should just avoid trying things about which we feel ambivalent. Slogans like "'I'm not sure' means no!" and understandings of consent that emphasize certainty, enthusiasm, staying within your limits, and getting full information in advance make our lives *smaller and narrower*. They cut us off from experiences and achievements we may find deeply fulfilling and deny us the empowering thrill of pushing our boundaries. Our autonomy is imperfect; sometimes we are unsure, divided, and anxious. Figuring out when and how we want to explore and take risks in such situations is a central part of self-determination and self-realization in the sexual domain but also in life more generally.

CHAPTER 6

Extractive Sex and Rape Culture

✖   ✖   ✖   ✖   ✖   ✖   ✖

Twenty-two-year-old Ken is horsing around with his friends at the pool. He dives into the water and his bathing shorts slip halfway down his ass. As he climbs out, one of his guy friends shouts, "Hey, no one wants to see that!" "My eyes are burning!" one of the young women jokes, "Cover that shit up!" The whole group laughs lightly, including Ken. Before he pulls up his shorts, he does a little sarcastic sexy dance for a moment, showing off his ass, and everyone laughs and groans, turning away and dramatically shielding their eyes. "Good thing you're going to be rich when you graduate," another guy friend calls out.

When I was a graduate student, I was asked to give a practice run of my "job talk" (the research presentation that an academic gives during an interview for a faculty position) in my home department. Afterward, the director of graduate studies, an older man known for his off-color comments, met with me to discuss how it went. "That was great," he said. "You gave a real 'fuck me' talk. That's what you want! You want to give a 'fuck me' talk." He grabbed the scarf that I was wearing and pulled it lightly against my neck.

"Wear this scarf for your actual job talk," he added. "This is a real 'fuck me' scarf." I expressed my annoyance about the conversation to a few of my fellow students and to one of my professors, but everyone's reaction was, "Oh you know how he is. He's incorrigible! He was just trying to say he liked the talk." It was impossible, though, for me to imagine him having this exchange with a male student whose talk he liked. I was too self-conscious to ever wear that scarf again. It never occurred to me to complain in any kind of formal way.

These two stories—the first fictional, the second factual—are not stories about rape. The first story, I hope, reads as a typical interaction between friends. The second is clearly what we would now count as sexual harassment, but without a threat of forced sexual activity. But both, I think, are good examples of how *rape culture* manifests and is perpetrated. In the first story, Ken is learning that as a man, it is normal to assume that his body is disgusting and an imposition, and that he will need other collateral, such as a high income or social status, to win women. Ken likely doesn't even experience this kind of joking around as insulting. By twenty-two, we all know that men's bodies are fair game for this kind of negging humor; it is just a normal part of socializing. The events in the second story underscored for me not only that my female body was presumed to be universally sexually desirable, but that I was expected to use that desirability as a social tool to help me get jobs or other social opportunities. My desirability was something to be weaponized, in ways disconnected from any sexual desires of my own. It also enforced the message that my body was fair game for being touched and grabbed without my invitation. Both these stories make up part of a pervasive web of small events that bit-by-bit entrench everyone within a toxic, gendered, heterocentric cultural economy of sex and desire that is extremely hard to resist or escape.

88   SEX BEYOND "YES"

People often throw around the phrase, "rape culture," but what does it mean, exactly? A simplistic interpretation is that rape culture is culture insofar as it encourages, normalizes, and tolerates rape, especially men's rape of women. But this is not very helpful. Rape is widely seen as an especially heinous crime, so it's not plausible that we have a culture that *directly* approves of, celebrates, or encourages rape. And although rape happens much more than it should, it is not a constant occurrence; we don't live in a culture where people just go around raping one another, so it can appear hyperbolic or sensationalistic to say we live in a rape culture if that's what is meant. Rape culture is instead best understood not as a culture that literally encourages or condones rape, but instead one that understands "normal" sexual (and especially heterosexual) relations as shaped by an extractive, asymmetrical gendered logic that is similar to the logic of rape. It offers scripts, norms, images, policies, and tropes that make rape explicable and reasonably cost-free and blurs the line between seduction and rape.

According to the commodity model of sex that Millar critiques, men need to extract sex from women, while women's sexuality is a valuable possession that they should try to hold onto until they can get the highest price for it. Within this commodity model, sexual negotiations are antagonistic. Sex is a win for men, and a loss for women, unless a woman strikes a good deal in which she is well compensated for putting out, with money, security, a child, or some other good. Intimately entangled in this model is the presumption that men are inherently sexually undesirable, that their bodies do not inherently provide the women they fuck with pleasure, and thus that they have to find some other way to extract sex from women. They must use their literal and metaphorical "purchasing power" or resort to trickery to get sex, since women would not independently desire to just give sex to them.

Correspondingly, women's bodies are inherently desirable. Women need to use their fuckable bodies as tools for negotiating with men, and they should not be surprised when men respond by assuming that they are offering sex.

This toxic sexual culture makes rape understandable, although not excusable. Men are taught that if they "play by the rules"—pay for dinner, promise to be monogamous, go to boring chick flicks on dates—then they have earned sex; women are "bitches" if they still turn them down after they have done what they are required to do in order to get sex through the proper, culturally approved channels. If a man feels like he has offered a "fair price" for sex, then it can feel like it's unjust discrimination or dirty dealing if he doesn't get sex back in return. It is not surprising, in this commodifying context, that men who think that they have been "nice guys" who played by the rules but did not receive "the goods" often feel angrily entitled to sex, and even are sometimes willing to rape women in order to just "take what is rightfully theirs." *Incels* are men who feel rejected by women and entitled to sex and blame women for their own failure to get sex, sometimes with terrifyingly violent results. They are pathetic and inexcusable. But when we frame sex as a bartering game with rules and tell men that their self-worth and value depend on their "winning" this game, the existence of incel culture becomes unsurprising.

This extractive picture of sex and gender relations frames regular, successful, romantic sex as having a logic similar to that of rape: men win sex from women via conquest, by getting them to give it up despite their reluctance or lack of desire. Men's persistence in pushing for sex is both necessary and part of romantic courtship and seduction. Even when men do not rape women, this model inculcates a rape mindset towards sexual relationships, according to which women's agency, desires, and pleasures are not of central concern for men, who are more interested in succeeding in getting sex one way or another.

Meanwhile, rape is typically the only sex crime that we imagine or talk about. We put the actual crime of rape on a pedestal, treating it as uniquely horrific, and engage in black and white thinking according to which surely nice, normal men couldn't have possibly done *that* horrific thing. Because of this, men who do not literally rape women, or at least believe that they do not, think of themselves as sexually blameless "nice guys," even when they try to coercively extract sex from women.

The extractive model of seduction and rape makes it hard for us to even imagine or articulate any kind of rape other than men raping women. But other kinds of rape are not uncommon. Black philosophy professor Tommy Curry, in his eye-opening 2017 book, *The Man-Not*, did an amazing job of documenting the long and hidden history of white women's rapes and sexual assaults of young black men and boys. US Department of Justice statistics show that queer and trans people are at sharply heightened risk for rape and sexual assault.

It is obvious that rape itself is a direct, extreme violation of sexual agency, by definition. But rape culture is poisonous to sexual agency even when rape doesn't happen. Rape culture restricts everyone's agency in the straightforward sense that any set of narrow and ritualized social scripts about how sex is supposed to go restricts agency, but it also harms both women's and men's sexual agency in distinct ways.

Rape culture harms women by denying them access to sexual desire and exploration, reducing their sexual agency almost entirely to the right to say "no." It teaches them that they must take up a constant defensive posture, cultivating a default stance of refusal, and moving carefully through the world so as to protect their bodies from men, whose job it is to try to extract sex from them. Just as people living in a gated community surrounded by passkeys and security cameras have less agency than those who feel able to wander their city freely, women lose agency by being trained to restrict their movements and securitize their bodies. Women's lives are shaped not just by rape but by the fear of rape, a fear that restricts their freedom.

While women are typically framed as the victims of rape culture, I am equally interested in how men's sexual agency and pleasure are seriously damaged by this culture. Rape culture harms men's agency by making it socially unacceptable for them to say "no" to sex or to explore their own desires with any subtlety. Whether or not a man happens to want sex at a given moment with a given woman, it is framed as "unmanly" for him not to try to "get some." I mentioned earlier that the medicalization of erectile dysfunction frames "healthy" men's sexuality as the ability to get and keep erections at will. This feeds into the assumption that proper, healthy men are always "up for" penis-in-vagina sex. Rape culture narrows men's sense of what their sexual agency is supposed to look like and then sets them up to be angry when that form of sexual agency proves elusive or unsatisfying. It also teaches men that their bodies are weaponized, feared, and loathed, which can hinder their capacity for joy in their own bodies. "Nice" men learn that they must control and self-monitor their own movements through physical and social space so as to minimize the apparent threat they pose to women.

The idea that men's bodies are inherently unattractive, gross, and to-be-hidden is the less discussed mirror of the much more familiar point that society treats women's bodies as universally appropriate objects of sexual attention and attraction. Male body shaming is so routine that we hardly notice it. Small penises are treated as laughable and gross, and large penises as intimidating and animalistic, and also still gross. We call penises "junk." Men in speedos and other revealing clothing are treated as a punch line rather than a turn on. When a man is accidentally caught naked, it's standard to make jokes such as "I can't unsee that." Fat men and hairy men are especially, but not exclusively, fair game. There exist male strip clubs for straight women, though of course not nearly as many as there are female strip clubs for straight men. But straight women almost always treat going to a male strip club as a kind of ironic gag requiring a lot of alcohol. A popular viral meme from 2023 shows one tweet that reads, "What's something that's hot in books but repulsive irl?" and a reply that reads, "men." In sum, it is culturally acceptable, even expected, to devalue men's bodies and treat them as repulsive.

We talk about and treat women's bodies so differently! Certainly, fat women, trans women, and "ugly" women are body-shamed mercilessly, but the default assumption is that "normal" cis women's bodies are appealing and attractive. Insulting a woman's body, which certainly happens plenty, presents itself as an openly hateful act, whereas men's bodies are insulted routinely in a "friendly" or "funny" way, with no recognition that this might harm. Most women, including very average looking women, generally cannot move through the world without men complimenting their bodies. But also, women routinely tell one another how great each other's bodies are, and praise one another's looks. When is the last time you saw a social media thread full of straight men boosting one another up by telling each other how hot and cute they look?

We know basically nothing, scientifically speaking, about how much damage it does to men's self-esteem or their ability to take comfortable pleasure in their own bodies to have all of society telling them that they are disgusting. But it makes sense that male body shaming plays directly into the hands of rape culture. In *The Right to Sex*, Amia Srinivasan talks about how women's bodies are treated as "supremely fuckable," but we need to discuss the equally intense messaging that men's bodies are "supremely unfuckable." We are quite used to talking about how the sexual objectification of women contributes to rape culture, but much less adept at thinking through how the shaming of men's bodies does as well. If you think that you are essentially physically unattractive, and that your body is an unwanted imposition, it follows almost immediately that you will need to get sex some way other than waiting for people to be naturally attracted to you and eager to do things with your body. It is no surprise, in this context, that men feel that they need to try to "buy" sex through offering other goods like money, status, or security, or trick women into sleeping with them through manipulation or coercion, rather than navigating toward sex by expressing attraction and building connection. It is also unsurprising that many men think that they should never turn down sex because they are lucky to get it. Conversely, if women are raised to think of men's bodies as gross, and of sex with them as not inherently appealing or fulfilling, then they will feel that they should agree to sex only if they "get something" in exchange. If men are consistently told that their bodies are not appealing sources of pleasure and gratification, it is unsurprising that they expect the process of "seduction" to consist of requests and (grudging) consent. Badgering or maneuvering women into giving into sex is often the best men feel they can hope for. It is not hard to see how all of this leads to a lot of barely consensual, often unwanted, bad sex for *everyone* concerned!

Mainstream heterosexual culture is not the only sexual culture around, of course. Gay men's communities famously worship rather than deride men's bodies and celebrate masculine beauty. But sexual subcultures that openly value men's bodies are treated by the dominant culture as perverse and abject. There is, for example, more homophobia directed at gay and bisexual men than at lesbian or bisexual women. At the same time, many gay men's communities happily appreciate masculine embodiment, but only when it meets extremely narrow and rigid standards for weight, fitness, body type, and race. Thank goodness, there are other queer communities that celebrate bears, otters, twinks, and all sorts of embodied masculinity. Indeed, in many queer-positive kink communities, it is standard to explicitly ban all forms of body shaming and to meaningfully embrace body diversity. But these communities are far from mainstream.

In 2024, a conversation flew around the internet: Women alone in the woods would supposedly rather run into a bear than a man. When this "news" was released, hijinks ensued. Women wrote serious threads about why they would prefer running into the bear: The bear is less scary and nefarious; people would not disbelieve a woman if she said she was attacked by a bear; the bear would not be creepy and annoying; and so on. Various outraged men provided statistics about how much more dangerous bears are than men. Unsurprisingly, those men were mocked for doing the exact type of mansplaining that made women pick bears in the first place. The man versus bear conversation positioned men as inherently predatory and women as inherently scared and vulnerable. Of course, the obnoxious mansplainers were technically right. The only sensible reason to pick the bear is that bears are so irresistibly fuzzy and adorable that it is hard to give up the opportunity to cuddle one, even if it means losing one's life. But, as is so often the case, when it comes to risk reasoning and social discourse, actual statistics were beside the point. The meme was ideological, not scientific, and its social function was to help further entrench an understanding

EXTRACTIVE SEX AND RAPE CULTURE

of the logic of gender as one of predator and prey, which helps make up the fabric of rape culture. Transfeminist scholar Julia Serano, in her essay "Nice Guys Finish Last," argues that being culturally framed as a predator restricts men's agency. She writes, "Just as it is difficult for women to navigate their way through the world, given the fact that they are nonconsensually viewed as prey, it is often difficult for men to move through a world in which they are nonconsensually viewed as predators. When I was male bodied, it was not uncommon for women to cross the street if I was walking behind them at night, or to have female strangers misinterpret innocent things that I said as unsolicited sexual advances."

Rape culture portrays the world, and especially cities and isolated places, as filled with dangerous male rapists who make streets and public spaces distinctively unsafe for women. This is a myth. In countries around the world, men, especially young men and men of color, are victims of violent street crime at dramatically higher rates than women. In 2022, 14,441 men were murdered in the United States, compared to 4,251 women. While our stereotypical image of violence between men is of a beef between gang members or drug dealers gone wrong, in reality, men are more likely than women to have experienced physical violence at the hands of a male stranger and more likely to experience violence from a stranger than from someone known to them. A recent Australian study showed that over a quarter of men have experienced physical violence from a stranger, with most perpetrators being male. Although more women are raped by strangers than men, stranger rape and violent rape in public space are extremely rare. Only about 17 percent of reported rapes of women involve stranger rape, and many of those are at campus parties and the like. The vast majority of rapes are not perpetrated by strangers on the street.

Despite the statistics, women are given the relentless message from nearly all directions, from childhood on, that they need to be fearful and cautious in public space, and that they must avoid being out alone, at night, unarmed, and so on. "Take back the night" marches, which have been held in multiple cities for decades, are premised on the assumption that women are at especially high risk if they are out at night. Women are trained to carry whistles and mace and to only travel with others. They are often encouraged to get self-defense training before navigating cities alone. The fact that men are actually physically at more risk than women from strangers on the street is in such sharp tension with our convictions about who is a predator and who is prey that I get nearly universal, sometimes even hostile pushback when I point it out, even though it is well documented and easily accessed via government websites around the world.

We should never minimize the violent and sexualized threats that men pose to women. But our distorted fascination with the dangers women supposedly face in *public space* is a way of controlling women's mobility, without protecting their safety. Ironically, all this training and messaging about the dangers of public space for women serves to increase women's isolation at home, the site of dramatically more common forms of rape and sexual coercion. Roughly one in five women are raped during their lifetime (although this statistic is very hard to measure and is probably an undercount) and ideological myths that keep them isolated at home and restricted in their mobility and access to community may well make the number of sexual assaults that actually happen higher rather than lower.

Of course, women do legitimately feel unsafe when they are out alone at night—they are trained almost from birth to be afraid. Men make the situation worse by catcalling, leering, and insisting on engaging women in creepy ways. But the reality is that the street is quite a safe place for women (as is the man-filled forest), while domestic spaces are often quite dangerous. Meanwhile, our unwillingness to acknowledge men's physical vulnerability to violence—the fact that they are not only the main predators but also the main prey—does them a grave injustice.

Extractive rape culture teaches men that they should be predators who tirelessly pursue women, since women will not naturally desire sex with them. Male characters in movies and television are celebrated for their persistence in trying to "win over" women, and for not giving up when women turn them down, finding ever more creative and flamboyant ways to break down their resolve to refuse sex. Men are taught that making refusal difficult is truly romantic, and a sign of their sexual prowess and masculinity. Meanwhile, women learn that turning a man down will be at worst greeted with anger or violence, and at best greeted with renewed, often exhausting, more intense attempts to extract consent from them.

Women are often exhorted to "just say 'no'" to unwanted sex. But often their potential partners make saying "no" awkward, socially costly, or hard to communicate. Often a refusal comes off as a humiliation or a rejection, and women are trained from childhood to avoid hurting people's feelings or risking men's anger. Our social norms around sexual communication are unsettled and ambiguous, so not everyone understands women's attempts at gentle refusals, such as "I am really tired," or "It was nice meeting you," in the same way. Refusal is made yet more difficult for women by the longstanding idea that women often say "no" even when they secretly want to have sex, as part of the game of heterosexual seduction. This trope can make it difficult for women's refusals to be heard as real refusals in the first place. It also blurs the line between rape and seduction by making it sexy to take refusal as a negotiable challenge.

We should turn the entire extractive logic of sexual negotiation on its head. It should not be men's job, or anyone's job, to extract a "yes" to sex by making refusal hard. On the contrary, good sexual negotiation that scaffolds and encourages agency makes it easy for everyone involved to refuse anything at any time. (We should also make it easy for people to say "yes," since many people, especially women, are trained up on the idea that they should never admit they want sex.) Good, ethical sexual negotiation is partly about making cost-free room for "no," and never about fighting one's way to a "yes," despite what Hollywood romcoms have told men to do for decades.

In a healthy culture of sexuality, it would always be easy and reasonably cost-free to refuse or accept sexual overtures. We should actively try to open up space for our potential partners to refuse. Lief and Icarus suggest establishing a norm of thanking people for saying "no" or putting on the brakes during sex, giving them appreciation for communicating well. A 2016 *Teen Vogue* article called "Everything That You Need to Know About Consent That You Never Learned in Sex Ed" points out that making refusal easy can be as simple as explicitly encouraging your partner to say "no" at any point, actively assuring them that you will not take a refusal as a personal attack or as an opening to argue the point. Just checking in during sex and asking, "Is this good? Do you want to keep going?" can create comfortable room for refusal. A nice perk of making refusal easy is that when someone does decide to have sex with you, you can be more confident that they did so out of desire rather than a feeling of obligation or social pressure.

I suspect that some men will worry that if they make refusal too easy, then women will always refuse, because they believe that they are inherently undesirable and gross and that women don't seek sexual pleasure. This is why we need to dismantle different parts of rape culture—extractive sexual negotiation, male body shaming, and norms telling women that they are not supposed to desire sexual pleasure—simultaneously. But in the meantime, trying to high-pressure people into having sex is not a good solution for anyone.

We may (or may not) be able to reduce the number of rapes with well-designed laws and policies, but that will never be enough on its own to dismantle rape culture because extractive sexual and gender dynamics are iterated, scripted, normalized, and enforced through songs, movies, platitudes we tell our kids, jokes, memes, and embodied habits that most of us are inducted into from childhood. I think our best hope is to attack rape culture through both thoughtful critique and the creation of alternatives, pointing out the toxicity and arbitrariness of the assumptions, products, and norms of rape culture whenever we can, and challenging ideologically loaded, toxic patterns of "joking" and regressive Hollywood narratives. At the same time, we need to be generating alternative scripts, establishing better norms of negotiation, and working to normalize better ways of imagining sex and gender relations. We need to understand sex as a joint, collaborative activity that should be driven by mutual desire and a shared quest for fulfillment and self-expression, rather than as an inherently antagonistic negotiation. Rape culture harms everyone's agency. Even those of us who are queer or nonbinary cannot entirely avoid the demands and expectations of heterosexual culture. Dismantling the scaffolding of rape culture—questioning its norms, replacing its scripts, figuring out when our policies and spaces support it, and rebuilding—will enhance pleasure and agency for everyone.

CHAPTER 7

Sex Work and Sexual Contracts

❋ ❋ ❋ ❋ ❋ ❋ ❋

*J*oe Gow, 64, and his wife, Carmen Wilson, 57, are both professors with long records of scholarly research publications and academic administration. Until recently, Joe was the extraordinarily successful chancellor of the University of Wisconsin–La Crosse, where he was well-loved for pulling the campus out of a financial crisis and boosting morale. Joe and Carmen have a hobby that they love: they make porn videos of themselves and post them on their OnlyFans channel and other similar subscription platforms. Many of these videos involve them cooking and eating vegan meals with porn stars and then having group sex with them. When Joe and Carmen's side hustle was discovered at the end of 2023, Joe was abruptly fired from his chancellor position via a unanimous vote from the university Board of Regents. The president of the board claimed to be "alarmed and disgusted" by the videos. Now in 2025, Joe is in danger of losing his tenured professorship as well.*

Sex work comes in many forms, including prostitution, pornography, sugaring (serving as someone's partner in exchange for ongoing financial support), stripping, camming (sexually engaging with someone over video for money), and any other kind of sexual activity that is monetized. Sex work poses an interesting set of questions and problems in the context of this book: On the one hand, I have been promoting the importance of sexual agency and self-determination. Insofar as people freely choose to perform sex work or to hire sex workers, I should be in favor of these forms of sexual self-expression and self-determination. On the other hand, I have been arguing against the commodity model of sex, and against contractual models of consent. But in the domain of sex work, commodification and contractual consent seem essentially built in. Consent in the domain of sex work is necessarily going to look a lot like the kind of bartering that I have argued cannot capture and promote good sex. My view is that sex work is always going to be ethically risky, but that with the proper scaffolding, it can be an empowering and ethical exercise of sexual agency. This scaffolding is, unfortunately, hard to come by in the real world. My focus in this chapter is specifically on the agency of sex workers, although the agency of people who hire sex workers or consume their products is also an important topic.

Some people think sex work is immoral and should be banned because it involves sex outside the boundaries of a traditional monogamous, long-term committed relationship. By this point, it should be obvious that I have no patience with this sort of thinking. I don't think that sex needs to be some sort of magical meeting of two souls who are permanently in love in order for it to be ethical, pleasurable, and valuable, so of course I don't object to sex work from any such angle. Other people object to sex work because they think it's inherently wrong to commodify people's bodies. This seems like an incoherent critique, given that dancers, construction workers, models, agricultural laborers, and many others get paid for the use of their bodies—indeed, since it is impossible to perform any work at all without using our bodies, arguably anyone with any job has a commodified body under capitalism. So, I don't take this critique seriously.

Others object to sex work because the industry is often exploitative and dangerous. This is a much more serious critique, and any discussion of sex work needs to grapple with this fact. But many sex workers provide erotic services for money because they enjoy it and find it fulfilling and consider their work an expression of their self-determining agency. When you think of a sex worker, the first image that comes to mind may be of someone coerced into the job via sex trafficking, financial desperation, or drug dependency and kept in it by a controlling pimp, fear of deportation, or a lack of other options. Joe and Carmen don't sound like the typical kind of people we have in mind when we talk about the ethics of sex work. But why not take people who are choosing this kind of activity against a background of love, trust, and security as our models of sex workers, rather than centering tragic cases of sex trafficking and other forms of abuse and desperation? For some sex workers, protecting their agency involves helping them get out of sex work. But for others, protecting their agency involves helping them stay in sex work.

I support sex work exactly and only insofar as it can be safe, nonexploitative, fully consensual, and expressive of the agency of everyone involved. I also support making whatever societal changes we need to make in order to allow a healthy, ethical sex work industry to flourish. But there are a number of barriers to this. Some of them come from regressive social attitudes and bad social scaffolding for sex work. Others come from the fact that consent and negotiation in the domain of sex work have a distinctive and challenging structure, which isn't going to easily map onto most of what I've discussed in this book. In sex work, people bind themselves with sexual contracts. That is, sex work generally involves a request for services, explicitly spelled out, and an agreement to provide those services for money. I have spent a lot of time criticizing the commodity model of sex, but in the case of sex work, sex (or the performance of sex, or sex assistance), literally *is* a commodity! We have been exploring how we can enhance sexual agency and pleasure by getting past that model, but now we need to think about how to protect agency within it.

We have seen many situations in which it is important for us to have easy, cost-free ways of backing out of sex. But this is in tension with the notion of contracted sex. If two people form a contract, according to which one person will pay the other in exchange for them having specific kinds of sex, then it doesn't seem like the sex worker can simply change their mind about providing services, any more than their client can simply change their mind about paying. There would have to be some kind of penalty for backing out of the contract. If someone has contracted and paid for work, then it is unfair for the worker to quit in the middle or to refuse to do what they were contracted to do. This is because contracts, by definition, institute *obligations*, which is one of the reasons that I have avoided using contractual metaphors in talking about sexual negotiation; it feels like there is something troubling about sex ever being an obligation! This includes sex in the context of a traditional marriage, where sex is often treated as obligatory; we ought to be disturbed by this.

Earlier we saw that sometimes it is important that we be allowed to back out of plans without consequences, whereas at other times, we should be held to our word. If I agree to pick up your kids from school when you're out of town, I can't just suddenly tell you that I am no longer in the mood! You can and should hold me accountable for this promise that I made to you and the obligation that I took on by making it. But sex seems to be a different sort of case, where we feel like we should always get to back out for any reason and without recrimination or accountability (although our would-be partner is allowed to be disappointed if we change our mind). Sex work is different from most sex, though. If a contract is involved, there has to be some cost to breaking the contract, otherwise the contract is basically fake, more like an idle prediction about what might happen than a settled agreement.

Moreover, formal contracts can have a rigidity to them that makes sensitive, responsive negotiation more difficult. Once a sex worker contracts with a client to perform a specific service or activity, it is hard to see how there is room for the kind of nuanced conversation and adjustments we have talked about. Earlier I compared good sexual negotiation to negotiation with a friend over taking a walk through a new city: chatting about where to stop for coffee, changing routes on the fly, letting our friend know when we are tired and ready for a break. Once there is an explicit contract, this kind of fluidity is much harder to manage.

These problems are not unique to sex work. Whenever we are contractually bound to perform some sort of intimate, embodied joint activity, these sorts of ethical hazards arise. If I am a health care worker attending to my client's bodily needs, for example, and I feel uncomfortable being around or touching that person, I can't simply bail on my contracted duties without consequence, but it is also disturbing to think that I could be trapped by a contract into intimately caring for the body of someone who makes me uncomfortable. We might think the same about a foster parent who is paid to care for a child, or a boxer who has contracted to fight someone they later feel unready to face. But we accept that people can contract to deliver health care, foster care, and professional fights, even though we might recognize that it is troubling to force people to deliver such intimate services if they are no longer comfortable doing so. On the face of it, the same should go for sex work. In all these cases, we should be especially careful to craft contracts that protect people's autonomy and bodily boundaries as well as possible, under the circumstances, given their special ethical risks. These contracts should include negotiated limits, expectations, and rules for renegotiation. Contracts for sex work and other intimate work should always include provisions for breaking the contract; although we saw that there needs to be some cost to getting out of a contract, no one should be forced to provide sexual services to someone else.

I've made it clear that I am no fan of the enthusiastic consent model of sexual agency. We saw how sex without enthusiasm can be a healthy expression of agency in cases of sexual generosity or ambivalence. Thinking about sex work gives us another way to see why it is important to separate enthusiasm from both consent and agency. Although sex workers are as capable of sexual enthusiasm as anyone, it is ridiculous to require that they be enthusiastic about every job they take on. In a wonderful 2013 column on the blog *Tits and Sass*, written by and for sex workers, prostitute Charlotte Shane writes eloquently about the pitfalls of conflating enthusiasm and consent. She actively prefers not to give "enthusiastic consent" when she is working because she wants to maintain some privacy and professional distance from her clients. Although she enjoys her job, she is not doing it for her own sexual gratification. But this doesn't mean that consensuality and agency aren't important for sex workers!

Shane insists,

> There is a stark difference between the times I've agreed to (undesired) sex with clients, and the times I haven't agreed to certain types

of sex with clients. Labeling all of those experiences "rape" erases the truth, my reality, and my agency. It also means, as many sex workers have pointed out when dealing with prohibitionist propaganda, that my "yes" and my "no" while I'm working are equally meaningless, so there would be no difference between my experience with a client who respects my boundaries and one who doesn't.

This is a crucial point. Folding together enthusiasm and consent makes it impossible for us to distinguish between someone who is raped and someone who has chosen for their own reasons to do something they are not wild about, which happens all the time. Of course, far too many sex workers are, in fact, nonconsensually coerced into sex, and this is a serious moral problem. But it is a moral problem that we cannot articulate or address if we conflate those tragic cases with the cases of sex workers who have freely chosen their profession and consented to sex with their clients, but who, realistically, are not melting with sexual pleasure during every job.

Joe and Carmen are lucky that they are so enthusiastic about their sex work, and it helps enormously that it is a side hobby for them. They make porn only when they happen to be inspired and excited to do so, although I bet that even they sometimes keep filming to finish a job, despite being tired and bored. But most sex workers, like most other kinds of workers, consensually perform their job even though they don't usually find it thrilling. Here as elsewhere, a lack of enthusiasm does not generally imply lack of agency or lack of consent.

In some ways, sexual consent functions quite differently from everyday consent to things that do not involve joint intimate activities. Sex work is challenging because it often inhabits a gray area between these two types of consent.

For example, although sex can be consensual without being enthusiastic, normally we think that sex needs to be actively embraced and self-determined in order to be consensual. But this is not so in other everyday consent situations. Imagine that you ask me whether you can borrow my bicycle. I say, "Well, I wish you wouldn't, I really would like access to it today and I also always worry about people borrowing it and messing it up, but if you really need it, okay." You say, "Yeah sorry, I really do need it!" And I say, "Fine!" and give you the combination to the lock, perhaps with an annoyed sigh. Under these circumstances, I think it is clear that I have consented to you using my bike, albeit unenthusiastically. If you take the bike, you have not violated me, although I might feel resentful. But if we now imagine having the analogous conversation about sex, it has quite a different feel! If I tell you, "I really wish you wouldn't have sex with me, I am actually not comfortable with it, but if you must, go for it," and I grudgingly take off my clothes with a resentful sigh, and you then go ahead with having sex with me, the problem feels much deeper than my lack of enthusiasm. If I've made it clear I am uncomfortable having sex with you and wish I didn't have to, then it's not cool for you to have sex with me. It is a violation of my bodily integrity and agency if you ignore my wishes and comfort.

Sex work seems to fall into a troublingly uncertain area between these two types of cases. If someone agrees to perform a job for money, then even if they make it clear they are not really into the job, it seems reasonable to continue to let them perform the work. This presumably includes sex work. At the same time, it seems to be disrespectful and distorted to want to have sex with someone who has made it clear that they are not happy about or comfortable with having sex with you, including if they are a sex worker. I don't think this situation would constitute a consent violation, but it does seem to be a disrespectful and agency-undermining way to treat people who are working for you, especially when the work they are doing involves bodily intimacy and vulnerability.

Here is another way in which sexual consent usually has a different character from regular consent: In everyday life, someone may have permission to do something without knowing that they have it. For example, imagine I put up a sign saying anyone is allowed to walk through my private yard. You walk through my yard even though you haven't seen the sign. It would be odd for me to complain that you did so without my consent. My sign permitted you to cross, whether you knew about the sign or not. More generally, you have permission to do all sorts of things you might not know about, such as use your local library, or take a tax deduction, or board a train without paying on a special day when fares have been suspended. But here again, sex works differently. If I make a public announcement on social media that Jason Momoa has a standing invitation to have sex with me, and then when I meet Jason Momoa, he helps himself to sex with me having not read my post, it seems clear that he has raped me, and that this is not what we mean by consensual sex. (Of course, the way this would probably play out in practice is that I would actually express delighted and surprised willingness to have sex with Momoa if he tried to initiate it, but then *that* would be my consent, not my public post.)

Why is sex different from walking across a lawn or boarding a train without paying? When I have sex with someone, it is a *joint activity*, and it is important to its being a consensual joint activity and not a violation of my body that we decide to do it *together*. This is possible only if we are communicating successfully. If it turns out that you were just lucky and happened to do something I was trying to give you permission to do, you were not acting out of respect for my agency, and we were not collaborating or negotiating. This is a consent violation, because consensual sex requires ongoing expression of the will to participate *and* ongoing recognition of and respect for one another's expressions of will. It is important, when thinking about sexual agency and other intimate embodied joint activity, that people care not just about their partners doing things that coincidentally harmonize with their will, but about their partners *actually respecting* their will, and this requires communication, and the communication has to succeed.

But again, sexual contracts in the context of sex work seem to be a gray area. If it's in your contract that you get to do anal with a sex worker, then, even if you don't know this, it seems off key for the worker to claim their consent has been violated if you do it. At the same time, you definitely shouldn't be having anal sex with anyone, including a sex worker, without checking to make sure it's consensual.

Sexual contracts, we are seeing, commodify sex, create barriers to exit, and simplify and flatten the negotiation process, removing some of its collaborative texture. How then can we ethically reconcile ourselves to sex work, if at all? I think the trick is to recognize that we cannot solve the ethical complexities of sex work (or for that matter, health care work or other intimate work) by simply writing really good contracts and insisting that they be respected. Rather, the scaffolding that surrounds these contracts can enable them to be localized expressions of agency. Good scaffolding—social, interpersonal, material, institutional, and economic—is essential to sexual agency, and sex work is no exception. Scaffolding that protects safe, ethical sex work includes normalized safe sex practices; destigmatization and freedom from bullying; strong communities of support for sex workers; financial security; access to health care; safe work environments; easy access to equipment and medications that reduce sexual health risks; a policing and legal system that penalizes abusers rather than sex workers; and so forth.

Without all this support, sex workers cannot negotiate good contracts freely as empowered agents, nor can they protect themselves if anything goes wrong. We need to make sure that only people who want to do sex work are doing it and that they have the option of quitting at any time. We need cultural norms and scripts that do not shame either sex workers or their clients, as it is harder to seek support and make good decisions when one is ashamed or afraid of being found out. In other words, as always, good negotiation cannot be the whole story and good scaffolding is key.

Within the context of strong scaffolding, we can make self-determining choices to bind ourselves by contracts that internally limit our autonomy and somewhat flatten our possibilities for negotiation. In fact, we do this all the time! When we rent an apartment, we agree to autonomy-limiting clauses, such as not being able to paint our walls or have pets or whatever. And it's not like we can engage in rich, ongoing negotiation with our landlords, generally. But even though landlord-tenant relationships very easily become exploitative, we do think it's possible to unproblematically express our agency by renting an apartment. Although here too, whether this is possible depends on the surrounding social scaffolding: how good the tenant protection laws are; whether there is a housing shortage; whether we have economic security. Sex work is intimate labor in which people are especially vulnerable to harm; but of course, having a secure living situation is also a pretty intimate core need. It is possible to freely and ethically enter into autonomy-limiting contracts that may end up harming us but that give us things we want. But this is *only* possible if we have background agency in virtue of being in a context that offers us power, support, resilience, and real choice.

In reality, sex workers are often at serious risk because of poor scaffolding. Many sex workers are financially or physically coerced into providing sexual services, out of financial desperation, fears of deportation, fear of a violent pimp, or other factors. Because of massive stigma and often criminalization, sex workers often have weak community support networks. They may not be able to seek help or exit a bad situation without risking being shunned, humiliated, arrested, or worse. Because they are often working under the table, they are frequently stranded without proper health care or other social benefits in places like the United States where these things are not universally guaranteed. But these are not problems inherent to sex work; they are problems that result from choices that we have made as a society about how to treat sex workers. The solution is not to further criminalize or demonize sex work, but rather to build better scaffolding. Some of this scaffolding already exists in some domains. For example, the porn industry has long standardized measures such as videotaped consent discussions, rules around establishing and respecting limits, and testing for sexually transmitted diseases. These are concrete measures that scaffold agency and safety. And there are communities both on- and offline made up of sex workers who enjoy their work and provide one another with scaffolding in the form of robust communities and support networks.

Someone who has meaningful choices and agency might decide to do sex work for lots of reasons. The most obvious one is that they may need money and find sex, or sex-related activities, a relatively fun and interesting or easy way to get it. They also might find getting paid for sex a turn-on or empowering. A different possible motivation is sexual altruism. There is a small movement to introduce sexual assistance and sex therapy for people with disabilities. In Germany and the Netherlands, sexual assistance is available by prescription. The motivating philosophy behind this movement is the idea that access to sexual pleasure and fulfillment is a basic human need and that making such access as universal as possible is a justice issue. This domain is fraught with ethical complications. For example, are we comfortable with someone who treats others poorly and hence cannot find sex partners trying to get themselves diagnosed with a "social disability" so that they can access sexual assistants? How could we safely gatekeep access to this service without overly medicalizing our social lives? And what should the rights of a sex assistant who is not comfortable with the needs of a particular client be? Regardless of where we come down on these interesting questions, it makes perfect sense that someone might pick a career as a sexual assistant because they are genuinely moved by sexual generosity and a commitment to sexual justice. We don't always have to have sex because of our own burning desire for sexual gratification; other reasons, including altruistic reasons, can be sufficient, as long as we have support and choice and are not being exploited or exploitative. Finding fulfillment and meaning in helping build others' sexual agency and giving them access to sexual pleasure is a comprehensible and legitimate reason to choose sex work.

Finally, some people choose to participate in sex work because it gives them pleasure, as a direct expression of their sexual agency. Joe Gow and Carmen Wilson would seem to be poster children for that group. I spoke with Joe and Carmen in-depth. It was clear that their decision to make and monetize pornography was about pleasure and self-expression. They are manifestly in love with one another, and find making and sharing the videos sexy, fun, and fulfilling. They have pseudonymously coauthored books about how porn enriches their relationship. When I asked them why they wanted to share the videos, they talked about how they enjoyed modeling loving, pleasurable sex between middle-aged people, as opposed to re-creating traditional porn tropes. Both Joe and Carmen discussed being sexually and emotionally gratified by the positive attention their videos received. Nothing in their story indicates the slightest whiff of coercion, abuse, or nonconsensuality. Although they did exchange sexual activities for (small amounts of) money, they were fully in control of the terms of their activities. This seems like the ideal circumstance for sex work.

Not only did Joe and Carmen make videos sheerly because they found it sexy and empowering, but also, on the surface of things, they seemed to have scaffolding in place that protected them from the normal risks of sex work. Both of them had prestigious and lucrative jobs, so they did not pursue sex work out of any kind of financial need. They have a loving relationship that includes good communication, as well as friends within the pornography industry that offer them community and help with navigating the world of sex work. Moreover, their videos are maximally wholesome, as far as porn goes: They are a committed, married, heterosexual middle-aged couple whose videos were not especially kinky, beyond the fact that several people were involved. If society is going to find any pornography ethically and socially palatable, this would seem to be the kind of porn that has the best chance. So, they seemed less at risk of social shaming and stigmatization than almost any other sex workers.

But despite their relative privilege, once they were involuntarily outed, it turned out that their scaffolding was not nearly as solid as they might have hoped or assumed. Not only did Joe lose his chancellorship and find himself under pressure to retire from the university altogether, but through a variety of social and material mechanisms, both Joe and Carmen were ripped out of their social networks and formerly safe spaces. Joe was barred from campus and allowed to retrieve his belongings from his office only with a police escort. This not only limited his motion but marked him as a threat and a criminal, isolating him from his community. Carmen lost access to her email and with it to her social media accounts, stranding her without access to friends and social networks. Joe's connections to others were scrutinized through what he called a "McCarthyist" investigation that made his attempts to reach out to anyone for advice or friendship precarious. All of these developments concretely undercut their agency, leaving them stranded without social support. At this point, their financial security is also at risk.

Sex work, in the right context, can be pleasureful, meaningful, self-determining, and fulfilling. It is not intrinsically incompatible with sexual agency. But in the world that we actually live in, it is fraught with ethical and practical risks. Although it is distinctive in various ways, like all sexual activity, sex work depends on good scaffolding in order to be safe and self-determining. This good scaffolding is unfortunately still hard to come by even under the best of circumstances. Even Joe and Carmen discovered in the end that sex work is socially risky. They clearly thought of their porn work as self-expressive and self-determining, but they turned out to be at the mercy of judgmental regents and alumni, and their videos took on social meanings they never intended or foresaw. So even in the best-case scenario, at present, sex work is vexed as a medium for sexual agency. When it comes to sex work, the scaffolding for even the most privileged and enthusiastic among us may be fragile. This is a social justice and infrastructure problem, not a problem concerning the morality of sex work itself.

CHAPTER 8

Domination, Submission, and Power Play

Max loves it when Lex uses toys from their shared collection to hit, cut, penetrate, and electrocute him, and he doesn't like to know in advance which toys Lex is going to use. Part of the fun of it, for him, is feeling like he has no control over what Lex is going to do to him next; he loves feeling at her mercy. But some days, Max has limits. For example, if he is going into the office the next day, he doesn't like to have visible cuts and bruises. Max and Lex have a system: the morning before they are going to play, Max leaves the toys that he is up for having used on him out on the dresser. Then Lex gets to choose what to use. This way, Max gets to have that hot feeling of being out of control and not having to negotiate in the moment, but he also feels secure. Max and Lex know one another's safe words just in case, but it's been years since they have needed to use them.

Stryker, a fifty-year-old man, likes to show up at kink events around town surrounded by his three "slaves," Baby, Bubbles, and Bambi, who are all women in their mid-twenties. The four of them live together and they have negotiated a permanent dom-sub dynamic: Stryker gets to decide who "his *girls" talk to and who they can have sex with. They ask for permission from him before they make social plans or spend money, and he chooses their clothing. If you ask any of them if they are happy with this arrangement, they will tell you that they love it. Each girl entered the polycule consensually and fully agreed to the terms of their relationship. They give seminars together on sadomasochism at kink conventions, in which Stryker teaches ways of safely beating the women. The women giggle with delight during these sessions and show off their bruises at the evening parties. They explain to curious outsiders that since they each freely chose this arrangement, with full information, it is empowering rather than subjugating.*

Submission can be super-hot. This fact troubles some folks, but it is a fact all the same. Current mainstream discussions of consent and sexual agency usually have little to say about domination/submission relationships and power play, beyond assuming that they are problematic. We are all supposed to want to be autonomous and in control. Twentieth century feminism taught us that women should be independent, just like men supposedly are, and that everyone should have exactly equal power. Yet not only are full autonomy and equal power elusive ideals, as we have seen, but many of us don't even want this!

It is important to think carefully about dominance, submission, and sex that plays with power differentials in the context of a book about sexual agency and good sex. Intentionally and enthusiastically giving up control and submitting to someone else is one of the most popular sexual activities out there. This includes domination and submission, sadism and masochism, bondage, humiliation, forced service, and other forms of power play. Most people within the kink community believe that all these tastes and activities *can* be ethically acceptable, as long as they are carefully negotiated in ways that protect the agency and well-being of everyone involved, but they can also be toxic and exploitative.

The desire to submit to a dominant partner is so common that it seems misleading to call it a kink. In fact, the majority of people—65 percent of women and 53 percent of men—fantasize about being sexually dominated. Humans are not the only animals that love and are skilled at power play. Go to any dog park to watch dogs exuberantly and voluntarily dominating and submitting to one another. But the popularity of submission and power play is puzzling on the face of it, since we typically associate agency with having power and control, rather than being at the mercy of anyone else's will or choices. Any satisfying exploration of sexual agency and good sex, in order to capture the full variety of human sexual tastes, choices, and pleasures, must make sense out of when and how submission and power play can be pleasurable expressions of agency.

Our exploration of domination, submission, and power play will focus on the world of kink and BDSM, which stands—awkwardly—for bondage, domination/discipline, submission/sadism, and masochism, but it can encompass any sexual practice that explicitly involves power play. This is for two reasons. First, power play is most directly associated, in most of our minds, with this world. Second, in kink and BDSM communities, the ethical and practical complexities of power play are explicitly discussed, celebrated, theorized, and negotiated. In actuality, domination, submission, and power play are common in all corners of the sexual universe. Many vanilla heterosexual couples assume that it is appropriate and sexy for the man to dominate and control a sexual encounter, and for the woman to be docile and obedient during sex. But this kind of power play is rarely made explicit or opened for ethical questioning. Kink and BDSM communities and practices provide us with invaluable resources for thinking about the tricky question of how to scaffold agency and enable pleasure in the context of submission and power play.

There is a stereotype out there according to which BDSM folks make use of a lot of formalistic, contractual language when they negotiate sex. In fact, Manon Garcia, in *The Joy of Consent*, claims that virtually *all* BDSM scenes involve actual signed contracts. This is not true. I have only seen literal contracts used a handful of times, typically when the people involved find the whole contract process itself erotic. But it is certainly true that this community is exceptionally interested in thoughtful and extensive norms of negotiation and the creation of spaces that scaffold sexual agency and pleasure. Unfortunately, many people now have access to all sorts of partial and decontextualized representations of BDSM, through porn and pop culture, without any immersion in the practices and concepts that that community has developed, and without the protection provided by the communal spaces it has built. This is a shame, not only because this kind of "amateur" BDSM lays people open to harm, but also because many techniques, concepts, and protections developed in the BDSM community would be helpful if imported to a more mainstream context.

It is by no means straightforward to explain when such power dynamics are part of good sex that expresses everyone's agency and when they are exploitative and oppressive. Sex involving domination and submission can very easily veer into ethically uncomfortable territory. Sometimes, power play is toxic and deserves criticism. But any account of sexual agency that cannot make room for the fact that huge numbers of people find sexual submission and power play pleasurable and self-affirming has a reality problem.

DOMINATION, SUBMISSION, AND POWER PLAY   119

Consider the two scenarios at the start of this chapter. I have seen variations of both of these situations countless times in the kink world. Your reaction might be different, but I find myself seriously uncomfortable with the second scenario and at complete ease with the first. The difference is not one concerning consent in any straightforward sense. Max gives up his right to consent or refuse, albeit in a limited, controlled way, but he has consented to the boundaries of this nonconsensual play. Stryker has explicit consent to treat his "slaves" this way, and they communicate ongoing enthusiastic willingness to continue this dynamic. Both scenarios involve people voluntarily giving up power and control and putting themselves in a partner's hands, and indeed, both involve inflicting physical harm. What are the relevant differences between these scenarios? Do the people in these stories have good, strong sexual agency? Why or why not? When is sexual agency compatible with submission and the voluntary relinquishment of choice and power?

I will start by defining some helpful terms that are standard in the kink and BDSM community and by giving a bit of historical context. A *scene* is a negotiated erotic encounter, which may or may not involve sexual intercourse. Kinksters are typically committed to negotiating the details of their sexual encounters, including how they will start and end, and so it is natural in that context to think of sexual encounters as defined scenes. The term also builds in recognition of the fact that kinky sex often involves some degree of theater. Any activity within a scene is called *play*. *Consensual nonconsent* refers to a consensual scene in which, inside the scene, one person has some license to do things to the other without their consent. A *dominant* or, more often, a *dom*, a *domme* (for femme people), or a *top*, is someone who takes up a position with more power and control during a scene, while a *submissive*, or a *sub* or *bottom*, is someone who has less control and power. The terms "dominant" and "submissive" are often conflated with "sadist" and "masochist," but they are different in meaning. A *sadist* gets erotic pleasure from causing pain, while a *masochist* gets erotic pleasure from experiencing pain. Typically, dominants give pain and submissives receive pain, but there is no reason why a masochist can't be in control and demand pain from a submissive sadist. Enjoying pain and enjoying submission are two different tastes, even if they often go together. Meanwhile, plenty of power play has nothing to do with pain or violence. Some subs like to be humiliated or degraded, or tied up, or to perform acts of service for their tops, or to be treated like an object or ordered around and used. While these are examples of relatively extreme sexual tastes, "traditional" sex often includes elements of these dynamics. Many traditional couples function as a dominant, "bossy" partner and a more passive partner who mostly takes orders, and many also enjoy playing around with light pain such as slaps and pinches, or with terms that flag power inequalities, such as "daddy" and "baby."

Kink culture has roots going back hundreds of years (and kinky activities are probably at least as old as humans, especially given that monkeys and apes use sex toys and enjoy oral sex and other nonreproductive sexual activities). Canonical books that formed our imagination of kinky relationships involving power play include *Philosophy in the Bedroom* and *120 Days of Sodom* by the Marquis de Sade, who was imprisoned in the Bastille for his views on sexual freedom before and during the French Revolution, and from whom we get the word "sadism" (although Sade was not much one for consent and should definitely not be taken as a sexual or moral hero of any sort); and *Venus in Furs,* by Leopold von Sacher-Masoch, from whom we get our word "masochism," written in 1870 in Austria about a willing male sex slave and his domme. More recent influential texts include

Anne Desclos's 1954 *Story of O*, written from the point of view of a submissive woman, and, unfortunately, E. L. James's 2011 novel *50 Shades of Grey*, about a BDSM relationship between a male dom and a female sub, which uncritically romanticized all the toxic behaviors and power dynamics, tired stereotypes, and agency violations that people in the BDSM world have long been fighting to excise from the community.

Kink culture, understood as a community and a collective lifestyle with distinctive norms and spaces, has its most important roots in Berlin in the early part of the twentieth century. Not only did pre-Nazi Berlin have a vibrant queer culture, but it hosted a network of not especially clandestine nightclubs, cabarets, and parties that celebrated kinky and queer sex. These early spaces for performances, scenes, and play provided material and social scaffolding for activities that were typically hidden. In these spaces, a set of norms, an aesthetic, a terminology, and a shared ethics of kink started to congeal, and specific sexual identities started to form. In the hundred or so years since kink culture arose in Berlin, it has expanded and developed. Today's kink world is populated by recognizable types such as leather tops, rope bottoms, brats (subs who like to act out and push their doms' rules), puppies (who are just what they sound like), cucks (who enjoy watching their partners have sex with other people), and many more, and people are always generating new kinks and kinky identities. There are now night clubs, parties, adult summer camps, meet-ups, and conventions for kinksters around the world, although Berlin remains Ground Zero for them.

Why do people want to practice power play and consensual non-consent? Why would anyone want to give away some of their autonomy, or let themselves be hurt, humiliated, or constrained? Conversely, are people who want to control, hurt, humiliate, or constrain their sexual partners just mean? There is no one-size-fits-all answer, but when kinksters are asked about what they like about power play, some consistent themes emerge. Both dominant and submissive folks usually say that the transgressiveness of this kind of play is part of its erotic thrill; it's fun to break rules and do things of which mainstream society disapproves. Moreover, it can be exciting to experiment with and temporarily adopt roles and ways of interacting different from those we inhabit in our everyday life. But dominance and submission also each come with distinctive pleasures.

Subs report that giving up control can be relaxing. Anecdotally, I've noticed that people who like to sub during sex often have a lot of responsibility in the rest of their lives and enjoy the break, finding it peaceful and even freeing to let someone else take control. For some submissives, offering sexual services and pleasure to a dominant partner can be a satisfying way of expressing care. Masochists often enjoy feeling strong enough to take physical abuse; it's common in kink contexts for masochists to proudly show off their cuts and bruises to demonstrate how tough they are. People who enjoy being humiliated or degraded during sex, similarly, often enjoy finding the strength to withstand the attack. Both subs and masochists may enjoy the attention that can come with being "adopted" by a top or a sadist. Many dom/sub relationships also make the sub feel nurtured and valued. Some subs report getting a feeling of security from being under the "protection" of a dom. And, for many folks, some kinds of pain or constraint just feel physically good.

Doms and sadists, for their part, may enjoy the feeling of control. Some doms talk about how they value their partners trusting them enough to let them take the lead. Like subs, many doms enjoy the attention they get from the relationship, and they may feel needed or admired by their subs. They may also feel empowered by their ability to provide pleasure to someone else. Some doms thrive in an orderly environment and find it easier to enjoy themselves if they can impose order. Sadists may directly enjoy inflicting (wanted, pleasurable) pain on their partners, which is honestly not that odd, if you consider how many of us enjoy combat sports, wrestling around with our siblings, and any number of other forms of constrained and consensual violence.

Sex is not the only context in which people regularly choose to give up some power and control. Lots of people like being "dommed" by their personal trainer, for instance, partly because it helps them achieve their training goals, but often also because they find it satisfying and pleasurable to cede this sort of control to someone skilled at using their power well. Many people like having mentors or coaches who tell them what to do. I often take pleasure in letting a friend "dom" me when I am on their turf; if I am visiting someone in their own city, I may let them choose where we go and what we see, or if I am eating at a restaurant with a friend who was brought up with its cuisine, I may let them order for me. This is partly just about acknowledging their greater expertise, but I also find it fun to put myself in the hands of a skilled friend who wants to give me pleasure. It can be enjoyable simply to relax into letting a master do their thing!

If I am going to voluntarily give up some of my autonomy, I need special guarantees that my partner understands my limits well and will respect them and safeguard my well-being. I also need to feel secure that I will be able to reclaim my autonomy when I need to. My partner and I need to negotiate a shared framework, within which I can safely abdicate some of my power and choice in sculpted ways. Max and Lex created such a sculpted container for agency with their system for leaving out toys. Another couple I met enjoyed playing at having the dom-

124   SEX BEYOND "YES"

inant partner penetrate the submissive partner while she "slept." They developed a code phrase: the submissive partner would say that she was "taking Tylenol PM and going to bed" in order to invite her partner to this kind of domination play (but please, never have sex with someone who is actually asleep!). In both cases, the point is to allow one partner to yield open-ended but limited sexual control to someone else.

A key premise of most power play negotiations is that everyone in a scene must be participating consensually, and this includes doms. Doms are vulnerable humans with limits, desires, needs, and the potential for trauma. It may be tempting, because of our traditional consent framework, to see the more submissive partner as the one with the job of rejecting or agreeing to what a more dominant partner requests. But in good negotiation, *everyone's* needs, pleasure, agency, and limits matter. We should never take a dominant partner's consent for granted.

It used to be a popular slogan in the kink community that scenes had to be "safe and sane," but now many people are critical of both those terms. The emphasis on "sanity" is arguably ableist: people with mental illness also get to be kinky and enjoy sex. And all sex comes with risks. BDSM is people's first association with "risky" sex, but any sex, including vanilla sex, risks not only physical injury but emotional harm and psychological trauma. We need to understand and manage risk, not avoid it. Some kinksters now instead emphasize *risk aware* consensual sex and recognize that being aware of risk never eliminates it.

Setting up exit conditions can be especially crucial during power play. Icarus recommends always asking questions in advance such as, "What happens if one of us hates this? How will we let one another know? Do we stop altogether? Or move to a backup plan?" When you voluntarily give away control over what happens to you, your requests to stop cannot be assumed to have literal force. Hence, other clear exit

DOMINATION, SUBMISSION, AND POWER PLAY 125

conditions (such as safe words or other agreed-upon signs) can protect agency. There are some forms of kinky play, however, where it is difficult or impossible to exit safely and quickly (consensually getting your penis locked into a chastity cage and letting your partner take the key to work, for instance). I don't want to claim that it is never wise or ethical to choose to do something from which exiting is hard or impossible. After all, outside of the sexual domain, we choose to get on amusement park rides that we can't get off until they end, or to get permanent tattoos. The inability to exit or reverse an activity is inevitably a compromise of our agency. But that doesn't mean we ought never to do these things. After all, agency is not the only value! Sometimes we sensibly compromise our agency for the sake of other goods, like thrilling experiences or beauty, but this is a weighty choice. If we are planning to try something that might be physically harmful, terrifying, traumatizing, or panic-inducing, we should be wary of not having a clear exit plan in place.

Aftercare is a word for how partners treat one another after a sexual encounter is over. Kinky folks widely recognize that whether someone experiences a sexual encounter as empowering and pleasurable or not often depends on how the whole interaction unfolds, and this interaction does not abruptly stop the moment literal sexual contact stops. The denouement of an encounter matters too. In negotiating aftercare, partners discuss how they want or need to be treated after the encounter. Do they want to be held and shown affection, or left alone, or perhaps to receive reminders that the power dynamic within the scene does not reflect their real-life relationship? Some people need specific sorts of verbal reassurance. Some people prefer that their partners stay for a while and hang out or sleep over, but others do not. It is odd that the concept of aftercare gets almost no uptake or recognition in the mainstream vanilla world, given that stories about people in effect getting aftercare *wrong* are rife in our culture. The guy who presumes that he can stay the night after sex when he is not welcome; the woman who wishes her date would cuddle; the guy who insists on doing the "gentlemanly thing" and walking his date home after sex, which actually creeps her out and feels condescending and invasive; the tales of someone having said the wrong thing after sex, or leaving too abruptly . . . all of these are familiar stories of sexual and romantic hurt, misstep, and frustration, so it's unfortunate that we have no mainstream tradition of discussing aftercare expectations in advance.

Thoughtful aftercare should be standard practice for everyone. But when it comes to consensual nonconsent, humiliation, or any other kind of power play, it is especially important that after the encounter, partners take time to build one another back up and make sure that everyone leaves feeling like a full and respected agent. Many kinky sex educators recommend that if someone gives their autonomy away during a scene, that autonomy should be explicitly restored afterward. There should be no ambiguity about the fact that the submissive partner is now a fully autonomous agent again, on the same footing as their partner. Long-time sex columnist Dan Savage introduced the notion of the "campsite rule": We should always seek to leave our lovers in better physical and emotional shape—happier, more empowered, more fulfilled and functional—than we found them, especially, but not only, when we have more power than they do. This should be an important principle when considering whether a scene is a good idea or not. I see no reason to restrict the campsite rule to kinky sexual contexts. It is a good goal for everyone to build their partners up rather than tear them down through sex.

We should also keep in mind that following the campsite rule requires not just that we treat one another well interpersonally, but that we build well-equipped campgrounds that have what we need to follow the rule. That is, agency in power play can be scaffolded not only by good negotiation, but by the material space in which it occurs. Spaces that are specifically designed for scenes at sex events and venues are called *dungeons*, *darkrooms*, or *play spaces*. In a (good) contemporary play space, rules are established for how to approach someone and invite them to participate in a scene, and how to respond if someone says "no." There are typically monitors or "awareness team" members who make sure that no one is invading anyone else's privacy or touching anyone without consent; that everyone is safe; that safe words are respected; and that no one is in distress. In well-developed play spaces, there are first aid centers and supplies in case anything goes wrong, as well as chill rooms where people who are feeling overwhelmed or need a break can escape from the action and not be approached. It is also standard for play spaces to provide tools for safer sex, such as condoms, cleaning supplies, and drop cloths to cover surfaces. More elaborate play spaces have rooms designed for specific kinks and types of role-playing; these often offer toys, sets, and props, and might include areas for medical play, fire play, or needle play, for example. Such spaces protect and enhance agency by making a wide range of activities possible and reasonably safe.

So far, I've been emphasizing what we can do to make power play ethical, pleasurable, and well-scaffolded. I have been pushing back against the common assumption that all such play is ethically suspect. But I don't want to be naively rosy about all of this: Power play can be genuinely harmful, or ethically or politically odious. I am in favor of letting people explore their kinks and be sexually adventurous, but that doesn't mean that there are no limits. Almost any kind of play is acceptable *if* it can be negotiated well from a position of genuine agency, and if at the end, everyone has agency and is treated with respect, but not all play is compatible with those conditions.

For example, an important criticism of power play, and of BDSM in particular, is that it is often complicit in toxic social norms. A lot of power play amplifies culturally pervasive sexist power imbalances, with women submitting to dominant, sadistic men. This sort of heterosexual dynamic makes me uncomfortable when I witness it, honestly. There are plenty of women dommes and sadists, queer doms and subs, and so forth, but the BDSM scene is still uncomfortably dominated by male doms with female subs whose dynamic mimics and amplifies traditional patriarchy. But even when a scene re-creates traditional sexist power inequalities, I am not ready to say it is automatically unethical. After all, a huge amount of traditional vanilla sex does this as well, only with less negotiation, less attention to consensuality, and less self-reflection. Very few people say that routine heterosexual sex in which men take the lead and women are relatively passive is simply unethical, so we should not have a double standard when it comes to kinksters.

But power play can only be ethical if the participants have enough equality and empowerment in their everyday lives that they can each negotiate from an agential position. A husband who already controls and belittles his wife regularly cannot ethically negotiate a scene in which he dominates her. She is already poorly positioned to exercise her agency or to refuse him, and she should not trust him to protect her agency during sex or to rebuild her autonomy afterward. As Lief and Icarus point out, power inequalities should not be in play during the negotiation stage. Although we live in a nonideal world in which power differentials are never totally absent, we should always do our best to create contexts and conversational norms that let everyone negotiate from as close to a position of equality as we can manage.

For this reason, I am deeply ethically suspicious of round-the-clock dom/sub relationships and master/slave relationships, where, by agreement, one partner gets to continuously control another partner's social activities, speech, meals, sexual activities, clothing, or other basic choices, even though these arrangements are not uncommon in the kink world. Remember the case of Stryker and his "slaves." Do these young women, especially against the background of misogyny and their age differential, actually have the social power they need to negotiate the terms of their treatment? Unequal power dynamics within a scene can be fun and fulfilling, but when there is no "outside" to the scene, there is no place from which the less powerful partner can negotiate on equal terms or call for an adjustment of the dynamic.

Likewise, I am suspicious of some forms of financial domination, an established kink in which one partner gives money to the other or lets the other control their finances and purchases. If the financial exchanges are small and playful, this can be fine. But if one partner does not have the financial means or freedom to exit the relationship, I don't think they can have agency within it. Again, notice that financial domming is common in the vanilla world; we just don't name it as a kink in that context. Plenty of couples have arrangements where one partner's financial dependence on the other is woven into their romantic dynamic.

A different sort of ethical hazard emerges when a scene might harm someone or some group who is not involved in it at all. For example, a consensual public humiliation scene might be super-hot for the people in it, but at the same time upsetting for passers-by who either don't know it's a negotiated scene or are harmed by witnessing that kind of humili-

130   SEX BEYOND "YES"

ation. A scene based on racial subjugation might be hot for participants, but unacceptably complicit in racist norms and cultural imagery.

Some kinds of kinky play involve role play, in which partners take up fictional identities and act out fictional scenes. Sometimes these scenes can get quite elaborate, involving costumes and set design: interrogation rooms with cops and perps, "furries" who dress up as animals, and so forth. This is different from, say, rope bondage, where you are not necessarily playing a role or creating a story, but rather literally tying someone up or getting tied up. Of course, scenes can involve both kinds of play—a BDSM scene might involve real whippings and floggings, packaged within a story about a schoolgirl being punished by her teacher for having done something naughty. You and I might agree that you *actually* get to order me around, within limits, during our scene. Or we might pre-script a scene together in which you *act out* ordering me around, while in fact we've decided together in advance what we will do. Both are legitimate and common forms of play, but it is important that everyone involved understand which one they are signing up for. A core ethical principle for role play is that you can negotiate a scene involving almost any kind of role play you want, but you *cannot role play during negotiation*. Negotiation always must be sincere and in good faith, and it cannot itself be a kind of pretend play; it must be for real in order to create the possibility of a scene within which role play is acceptable. Discussions about boundaries, limits, safe words, triggers, and so forth cannot themselves be a form of play-acting.

The line between role-play and playing "as oneself" is not a crisp one. Lots of people use role-play to try on an identity with which they are experimenting, or which they feel unsafe inhabiting in their everyday lives. For example, it is not uncommon to role-play by adopting a gender presentation different from one's everyday gender. This might be just a fun, hot game; or it may be a way of exploring whether one would be more comfortable with a different gender; or it can be an outlet for a fluid gender identity; or it can be a relatively safe way to express an authentic gender identity that one does not feel comfortable expressing in daily life. The boundaries between role-play and these other, subtler kinds of identity expression are not always rigid or clear, perhaps even to the person taking them up.

This can get complicated. In a gender-swap scene, for example, one person might think that it's all role-play while another might be expressing what they take to be their authentic gender. When we agree to sex, we are not just agreeing to an activity, but to an activity *with someone in particular*. It may strain the consensuality of an encounter if different people have conflicting understandings of *who* they are playing with and how they are playing. But in the fluid and nonliteral world of sex, it is not always easy to pin down what counts as pretending to be someone that one is not. It's also not clear what the boundaries of privacy are; in different contexts, people have different duties to disclose personal facts about themselves. Having sex does not give anyone an unlimited right to know everything about you. Tom Dougherty, in their influential article, "Sex, Lies, and Consent," argues that if one partner doesn't know something about the other that would have been a "dealbreaker"—that is, they would not have agreed to sex if they'd known about it—then the sex is not actually consensual. For example, if I would never knowingly agree to sleep with someone in the military, then if you don't mention to me that you are enlisted, my sex with you cannot be consensual. This seems harsh to me. We can't guess all of one another's dealbreakers, as Dougherty acknowledges. If we are having delightful hookup sex and plan to then go our separate ways, it seems to me that we can both be doing something we desire and freely choose, even if we would have made a different choice with different information. We are each choosing to have sex with someone we know little about, with all the risks that entails. But if I am building a long-term relationship with someone and I am deceived about who they really are, then this is a real compromise of my agency. I think we need notions of "good enough" consensuality and disclosure that is suited to the actual, imperfect world. Not every case of good sex involves deep mutual comprehension. Sex can be shallow and transactional but fun and fulfilling. But it cannot come at the cost of anyone's basic self-determination.

POWER PLAY, CONSENSUAL NONCONSENT, BDSM, and role play are all practices that can expand agency and bring joy and sexual fulfillment, but only with careful negotiation and good scaffolding. But this is true of sex in general, as we have seen. As a society, we should be building up people's negotiation skills and normalizing good negotiation practices. At least as importantly, we need to be thinking about how we create social, material, and institutional scaffolds that support rather than undermine sexual agency and pleasure. This requires reforming our legal system; working to eliminate sexual and body shaming, bullying, and pressures toward secrecy; building up community support; improving our sexual education and health care systems; making sure everyone has enough financial and housing security to not be dependent on any one relationship for their own survival and well-being; and building physical spaces for sex that give everyone access to privacy, safety, self-expression, and community oversight. It means reforming working conditions for sex workers. It also means understanding that edgy, risky, and ambivalent sexual choices can increase sexual agency, fulfillment, and pleasure, so we should not be discouraging them but rather making sure they are especially well-scaffolded.

We have seen that we rarely have perfect autonomy, but also that sex without perfect autonomy can be fun, consensual, exciting, and agency-enhancing. Icarus pointed out to me that, on the one hand, when it comes to consent and autonomy, "Nuance has always been a place for predators to hide," but on the other hand, nuance is unavoidable. If we insist that only perfectly autonomous, enthusiastic sex free of all power dynamics is acceptable, then people will not be able to explore, play, and express themselves in ways that can bring deep pleasure and fulfillment. Indeed, many people will be shut out of sex altogether.

We've explored how to build frameworks within which people can enjoy sexual agency and fulfillment. I've talked about how this can go wrong, but also about the many ways to make it go right. The power *to do* things is as central to freedom and agency as the power to prevent or avoid things. We should not base our entire sexual ethics on the precautionary principle of preventing abuse and harm, even though such prevention is of course important. If we do, we will end up with a fear-based sexual ethics that is fundamentally organized around saying "no" to sex and narrowing the range of our possible actions and experiences. I've tried to build a picture in which *everyone's* sexual agency matters, including people who are often left out of our sexual storytelling. I have also explored how we can protect and buttress our own and one another's agency even when we do not have perfect autonomy and are enmeshed in power relationships. Ultimately, my take-home message is that it is dreary and insufficient merely to focus on ensuring that all the sex that happens is consensual. We should build a sexual ethos and a social world in which sex can be not only self-determined, but also shame-free, empowering, exciting, and pleasurable for everyone.

ACKNOWLEDGMENTS

This book is the outgrowth of decades of endless discussions with friends, lovers, fellow academics and students, sex workers, sex educators, disability advocates, and fellow queer and trans kinksters. There is no way to thank them all. I am especially grateful to Jason Arroll, Ray Briggs, Tom Dougherty, Cassie Herbert, Eli Kukla, Celeste Ritchie, Camila YaDeau, and kinky sex educators Princess Kali, Frozen Mersault, and Icarus for shaping my thinking through in-depth discussions. Audiences at Cambridge University, Ludwig Maxmillian University of Munich, Northwestern University, University of North Carolina, Simon Fraser University, and Wayne State University provided wonderful feedback on various ideas that ended up in this book. I am grateful to the Alexander von Humboldt Foundation for research funding that supported various stays in Germany, where many of my ideas about sexual agency and pleasure have been formed. I owe a special thank you to my department chair, Mark Murphy, for suffering through my various rounds of asking the Philosophy Department at Georgetown to pay for me to attend kink conventions, sex toy exhibitions, and other events outside the academic norm, while rolling his eyes only internally. My most intense gratitude goes to my brilliant and infinitely supportive and patient partner, Dan Steinberg, who not only reads and helps me edit every word I write and discusses all my ideas with me, but who has reflectively and joyfully explored sexual agency and pleasure with me for well over a decade.

NOTES

CHAPTER 1: BEYOND CONSENT

4 **examples of bad sex, rape, misogynist violence, and consent gone wrong:**
Some examples of recent feminist books on sex that start this way include
Katherine Angel, *Tomorrow, the Sex Will Be Good Again: Women and Desire
in the Age of Consent* (Verso, 2022); Nicola Garvey, *Just Sex? The Cultural
Scaffolding of Rape* (Routledge, 2018); and Amia Srinivasan, *The Right to Sex*
(Bloomsbury, 2022). Kate Manne's *Down Girl: The Cultural Logic of Misogyny*
(Oxford University Press, 2017), is not a book primarily about sex, but it is
a prominent book that is particularly relentless in opening with examples of
sexual violence and sex gone wrong. Even Manon Garcia's book, *The Joy of
Consent: A Philosophy of Good Sex* (Harvard University Press, 2023), which
explicitly claims to focus on good sex, begins with rape and only gets to the
conditions enabling good sex in the final chapter.

6 **Less than 50 percent of Generation Z . . . identifies as cisgender and heterosexual:** See, for instance, Zing Tsjeng, "Teens These Days Are Queer AF,
New Study Says," *Vice*, March 10, 2016.

8 **consent as a collaborative project:** For example, in *The Joy of Consent*, feminist philosopher Manon Garcia defines consent as a collaborative conversation instead of an asymmetrical exchange, while sex educator and sex worker
Betty Martin, in her book *The Art of Receiving and Giving: The Wheel of Consent* (Luminare Press, 2021), defines it as an achieved agreement that people
design together.

11 **"women receive and vet proposals"**: Garcia, *The Joy of Consent*, **118.**

12 **releasing someone from the obligation not to do something to you:** Some
examples include Tom Dougherty, "Sex, Lies, and Consent," *Ethics* 123, no.

138   NOTES

4 (2013): 717–44; Hallie Liberto, "Intention and Sexual Consent," *Philosophical Explorations* 20, sup. 2 (2017): 127–41; and Victor Tadros, "Consent to Sex in an Unjust World," *Ethics* 131, no. 2 (January 2021).

14   **the tea analogy is distorting in its simplicity:** See particularly an excellent 2015 blog post by Justin Hancock on bishtraining.com called, "Have you seen that tea and consent video?"

15   **"In this 'commodity model,' sex is like a ticket":** Thomas MacAulay Millar, "Towards a Performance Model of Sex," in *Yes Means Yes! Visions of Female Sexual Power and a World Without Rape*, eds. Jaclyn Friedman and Jessica Valenti, editors (Seal Press, 2008), 30.

16   **"Your body is a savings account":** Josh McDowell, *Why Wait? What You Need to Know About the Teen Sexuality Crisis* (Here's Life Publishers, 1987), 304.

16   **"In the absence of affirmative participation, there is no collaboration.":** Millar, "Towards a Performance Model of Sex," 38.

CHAPTER 2: SEX TALK

23   **settling whether sex is going to happen and how it is going to go:** Manon Garcia, in *The Joy of Consent: A Philosophy of Good Sex* (Harvard University Press, 2023), suggests that we call all this communication "erotic conversation," to get away from any suggestion that sexual decision-making paradigmatically involves barter and compromise. But I think "conversation" is too broad. Strippers and cam girls, for instance, may have erotic conversations with clients, but these may not be sexual negotiations. Also, not all negotiation is verbal; we may navigate our way into and through sex in part via gesture and facial expression. We can use our bodies to express pleasure and discomfort, but also to invite, seduce, warn, slow things down, and much more. So, I will stick with "negotiation."

27   **speech act theory:** Speech act theory has its origins in mid-twentieth-century philosophy of language, and especially in the work of Ludwig Wittgenstein, Paul Grice, and J. L. Austin.

27   ***order* people to do things:** It is almost never ethical to order someone to do anything sexual. The only exception is orders in the context of a consensual and carefully negotiated dominance-submission relationship. We will talk about those later on.

28   **sexual promises are never appropriate:** See for example philosopher Haillie

NOTES 139

Liberto's argument against all sexual promises, in "The Problem with Sexual Promises," *Ethics* 127, no. 2 (January 2017): 383–414.

32 **Our social norms around gift-giving are complex:** Twentieth-century social scientists such as Claude Lévi-Strauss and Pierre Bourdieu were fascinated by gift-giving, both because of the complexity of its norms, and because of its important role in sustaining and negotiating community. As John Sherry explores in his classic article "Gift-Giving in Anthropological Perspective," *Journal of Consumer Research* 10. no. 2 (September 1983): 157–68, different sorts of gifts and different kinds of uptake and reciprocation are appropriate for a business associate, a hospitalized friend, a bachelor party, a lover, a wedding, a child's birthday party, and so forth.

CHAPTER 3: SCAFFOLDING GOOD SEX

46 **no one ever *owes* anyone else sexual interest, no matter what:** See Amia Srinivasan's powerful discussion of this in her essay "The Right to Sex," reprinted in her book, *The Right to Sex: Feminism in the Twenty-First Century* (Farrar, Straus and Giroux, 2021).

47 **Heterosexual, vanilla sex tends to follow highly constrained scripts:** See, for instance, the discussion of these constrained scripts in Kathryn Rittenhour and Michael Sauder, "Identifying the Impact of Sexual Scripts on Consent Negotiations," *Journal of Sex Research* 61, no. 3 (March–April 2024): 454–65.

48 **"a chain of events fully scripted and oriented towards men's pleasure":** Manon Garcia, *The Joy of Consent: A Philosophy of Good Sex* (Harvard University Press, 2023), 172–3.

48 **learning how to have sex by watching mainstream porn is like learning how to drive only through watching *Fast and Furious* movies:** Thanks to Eli Kukla for the vivid metaphor.

49 **relationship escalator:** See Gahran's original blog post at offescalator.com, as well as her book, *Stepping Off the Relationship Escalator: Uncommon Love and Life* (Off the Escalator Enterprises, 2017).

CHAPTER 4: IMPERFECT AUTONOMY

53 **Henry Rayhons was arrested for purportedly having sex with his wife:** Pam Belluck, "Sex, Dementia, and a Husband on Trial at Age 78," *New York Times* April 13, 2015.

140 NOTES

54 **unreachable and unhelpful fantasy:** I am not the first one to point out that this ideal of the fully autonomous self is unrealistic, and a hopeless starting point for understanding the standards for consensual sex. For example, Manon Garcia makes this point in her 2023 book *The Joy of Consent: A Philosophy of Good Sex* (Harvard University Press, 2023), as does Joseph Fischel in *Screw Consent: A Better Politics of Sexual Justice* (University of California Press, 2019).

55 **focus on sexual agency, not sexual autonomy:** Deborah Tuerkheimer, "Sex Without Consent," *Yale Law Journal* 123, no. 355 (2013): 335–52.

56 **minimal autonomy:** See Agnieszka Jaworska, "Caring, Minimal Autonomy, and the Limits of Liberalism," in *Naturalized Bioethics: Toward Responsible Knowing and Practice*, eds. Hilde Lindemann, Marian Verkerk, and Margaret Urban Walker (Cambridge University Press, 2008).

57 **"An intoxicated person cannot give consent":** From the University of Tulsa website. Many universities have similar statements on their websites.

57 **the intersection of alcohol and sex in their lives:** See Trevor Goodyear, John L. Oliffe, Hannah Kia, Emily K Jenkins, and Rod Knight, "'You Kind of Blame It on the Alcohol, But . . . ': A Discourse Analysis of Alcohol Use and Sexual Consent Among Young Men in Vancouver, Canada," *Health* 2023. This study built on my earlier work on nonideal autonomy.

60 **Dementia is associated with an increase in libido in 14 percent of people:** Evelyn M. Tenenbaum, "To Be or to Exist: Standards for Deciding Whether Dementia Patients in Nursing Homes Should Engage in Intimacy, Sex, and Adultery," *Indiana Law Review* 42, no. 3 (2009), is a good source for these facts and statistics.

62 **Hilde Lindemann's notion of "holding in personhood":** Hilde Lindemann, *Holding and Letting Go: The Social Practice of Personal Identities* (Oxford University Press, 2014).

64 **Even patients who are quite powerful in everyday contexts often feel disempowered in a medical setting:** This was the theme of the brilliant play, *Wit*, about a confident and successful professor dying of ovarian cancer. *Wit* was written by Margaret Edson in 1995 and adapted into an Emmy-award-winning television film on HBO starring Emma Thompson in 2001.

65 **I don't think such policies are sufficient to erase worries about those relationships:** Consensuality is not the only ethical issue when it comes to sex and relationships. A sexual relationship can be consensual and still be a bad idea. For example, a faculty member and a graduate student may have a gen-

NOTES 141

uinely consensual relationship, if proper supports are in place. Yet the relationship may be distorted in unhealthy ways by their unequal power and their different career stages, and their desires may be distorted by the lure of status or the fetishization of youth. The relationship may even harm other people, for example, if it messes up the social ecology of their academic department, creating suspicions of favoritism, toxic gossip, or a lot of discomfort among others who must manage the situation. I am loath to say that such relationships are automatically nonconsensual, but they may still be a bad plan even if they are consensual.

66 **patriarchy is structured by norms that demand that women serve men's needs:** Kate Manne argues this in *Down Girl: The Logic of Misogyny* (Oxford University Press, 2019).

66 **women could never have consensual heterosexual sex under patriarchy:** This claim was common during the second-wave feminism of the mid- to late-twentieth century, but it is most explicit and most typified in Andrea Dworkin's book *Intercourse* (Free Press, 1987).

68 **"create conditions for equality":** Garcia, *The Joy of Consent*, 205.

69 **Anna Stubblefield:** For a good overview of the Stubblefield case, see Daniel Engber, "The Strange Case of Anna Stubblefield," *New York Times*, October 25, 2015. A 2023 documentary, "Tell Them You Love Me," directed by Nick August-Perna, explores the case.

70 **"This is the action not of a sexual predator but of an honest and honorable woman in love":** Jeff McMahan and Peter Singer, "Who Is the Victim in the Anna Stubblefield Case?," *New York Times*, April 3, 2017.

71 **D.J.'s hypothesized pleasure is not the issue; his total subjugation to Stubblefield is:** Singer and McMahan claimed that if D.J. could not understand consent, then he was not harmed in virtue of not consenting. I think this is a deeply ableist view that would also justify sexually pleasuring infants, for example, and I consider agency and consensuality for everyone involved an absolute minimum standard for ethical sex. Singer has recently shown sympathy with the view that bestiality is acceptable as long as the animal finds the experience pleasurable, using a similar argument.

CHAPTER 5: AMBIVALENCE AND AGENCY

84 **kink educators and performers Lief and Icarus:** You can find out more about Lief and Icarus at their website, houseofbound.com.

142   NOTES

CHAPTER 6: EXTRACTIVE SEX AND RAPE CULTURE

90   **hard for us to even imagine or articulate any kind of rape:** Julia Serano writes, "the predator/prey mindset essentially ensures that men cannot be viewed as legitimate sexual objects, nor can women be viewed as legitimate sexual aggressors. This has the effect of rendering invisible instances of man-on-man and woman-on-woman sexual harassment and abuse, and it makes the idea of woman-on-man rape utterly inconceivable." "Nice Guys Finish Last," in *Yes Means Yes! Visions of Female Sexual Power and a World Without Rape*, eds. Jaclyn Friedman and Jessica Valenti (Seal Press, 2008), 230.

90   **white women's rapes and sexual assaults of young black men and boys:** See Tommy J. Curry, *The Man-Not: Race, Class, Genre, and the Dilemmas of Black Manhood* (Temple University Press, 2017).

92   **one tweet that reads, "What's something that's hot in books but repulsive irl?" and a reply that reads, "men":** From Twitter/X, reposted by Intergalactic Space Garbage, September 29, 2023.

93   **women's bodies are treated as "supremely fuckable":** Amia Srinivasan, *The Right to Sex: Feminism in the Twenty-First Century* (Farrar, Straus and Giroux, 2021), 104. Srinivasan claims this is true of "all" women's bodies, but I think she is not considering here how culturally desexualized and stigmatized trans women's, older women's, fat women's, and disabled women's bodies are.

94   **narrow and rigid standards for weight, fitness, body type, and race:** This is a much-discussed cultural phenomenon. See, for instance, Brandon Andrew Robinson, " 'Personal Preference' as the New Racism: Gay Desire and Racial Cleansing in Cyberspace," *Sociology of Race and Ethnicity* 1, no.2 (2015).

95   **difficult for men to move through a world in which they are nonconsensually viewed as predators:** Serano, "Nice Guys Finish Last," 231.

95   **14,441 men were murdered in the United States, compared to 4,251 women:** I got this figure from statista.com in 2024.

95   **over a quarter of men have experienced physical violence from a stranger:** Australian Bureau of Statistics, "Personal Safety, Australia" March 15, 2023, https://www.abs.gov.au/statistics/people/crime-and-justice/personal-safety -australia/latest-release.

95   **Only about 17 percent of reported rapes of women involve stranger rape:** This statistic is from the National Sexual Violence Resource Center, but it is widely repeated. In general, the National Sexual Violence Resource Center

NOTES   143

and the Department of Justice are good sources of statistics on gender, rape, and violent crime in the United States.

97 **difficult for women's refusals to be heard as real refusals in the first place:** Feminist legal theorist Catharine MacKinnon and feminist philosopher Rae Langton have both argued in detail that our culture makes it hard for women to successfully perform the speech act of refusing sex.

99 **Dismantling the scaffolding of rape culture:** Legal scholar Nicola Gavey has argued that everyday forms of heterosexual culture "scaffold rape." See her book, *Just Sex? The Cultural Scaffolding of Rape* (Routledge, 2005).

CHAPTER 7: SEX WORK AND SEXUAL CONTRACTS

106 **" . . . there would be no difference between my experience with a client who respects my boundaries and one who doesn't":** Charlotte Shane, "'Getting Away' with Hating It: Consent in the Context of Sex Work," *Tits and Sass*, March 21, 2013.

107 **I think it is clear that I have consented to you using my bike:** I have adapted this example, and the next one involving walking across someone's lawn, from examples given by Tom Dougherty in their book, *The Scope of Consent* (Oxford University Press, 2021).

CHAPTER 8: DOMINATION, SUBMISSION, AND POWER PLAY

116 **forms of power play:** Such power play is often called *power exchange*, which I find misleading, since these practices are not about trading power around but about intentional power asymmetry.

117 **65 percent of women and 53 percent of men—fantasize about being sexually dominated:** See Christian C. Joyal, Amélie Cossette, and Vanessa Lapierre, "What Exactly Is an Unusual Sexual Fantasy?" *Journal of Sexual Medicine* 12, no. 2 (February 2015): 328–40. These authors only gave their research participants the choice of identifying as men or as women, so we have no data for nonbinary folks.

118 **BDSM scenes involve actual signed contracts:** Manon Garcia, *Joy of Consent: A Philosophy of Good Sex* (Harvard University Press, 2023), 68.

118 **partial and decontextualized representations of BDSM:** Stacey May Fowles makes this point in "The Fantasy of Acceptable 'Non-Consent': Why the Female Sexual Submissive Scares Us (and Why She Shouldn't)," in *Yes*

144   NOTES

Means Yes! Visions of Female Sexual Power and a World Without Rape, eds. Jaclyn Friedman and Jessica Valenti (Seal Press, 2008).

119 **a *top* is someone who takes up a position with more power and control during a scene, while a . . . *bottom* is someone who has less control and power:** "Topping" and "bottoming" can also be used to mean penetrating and being penetrated, respectively. This is a quite different issue from that of who has more power, so these terms are problematically ambiguous. I will use them to mean the same as "domming" and "subbing." I don't generally find the topic of who is using an outie and who is using an innie especially interesting.

131 **they would not have agreed to sex if they'd known about it:** Tom Dougherty, "Sex, Lies, and Consent," *Ethics* 123, no. 4 (July 2013): 717–44.

READINGS IN CONVERSATION

CHAPTER 1: BEYOND CONSENT

Fischel, Joseph, *Screw Consent: A Better Politics of Sexual Justice*. University of California Press, 2019. Fischel argues that consent is overemphasized in our discussions of sexual ethics and politics.

Friedman, Jaclyn, and Jessica Valenti, eds. *Yes Means Yes! Visions of Female Sexual Power and a World Without Rape*. Seal Press, 2008. A classic collection of essays exploring the notion of affirmative consent and promoting a sex-positive feminism.

Garcia, Manon. *The Joy of Consent: A Philosophy of Good Sex*. Harvard University Press, 2023. Garcia discusses the importance of conversations to good sex and argues that our traditional understanding of consent has been too narrow.

Millar, Thomas MacAulay. "Towards a Performance Model of Sex," in *Yes Means Yes!*. Millar explores and critiques the commodity model of sex and proposes the performance model as a more ethical and fulfilling approach.

Woodard, Elise. "Bad Sex and Consent." In *The Palgrave Handbook of Sexual Ethics*, ed. David Boonin. Palgrave Macmillan, 2022. Woodard argues that our narrow focus on consent has obscured the many other ways in which sex can go badly.

146   READINGS IN CONVERSATION

CHAPTER 2: SEX TALK

Kukla, Rebecca. "That's What She Said: The Language of Sexual Negotiation." *Ethics* 129, no. 1 (2018). I develop my account of how different sorts of speech acts can contribute to sexual negotiation.

Liberto, Hallie. "The Problem with Sexual Promises." *Ethics* 127, no. 2 (January 2017). Liberto argues that making promises during sex always overcommits the promiser and that we should never hold people to sexual promises.

Martin, Betty. *The Art of Giving and Receiving: The Wheel of Consent*. Luminare Press, 2021. Martin, an influential sex educator, introduces the "Wheel of Consent" framework, highlighting different kinds of consent and advocating for understanding it as an ongoing dialogue between partners.

Williams, D. J., Jeremy N. Thomas, Emily Prior, and M. Candace Christensen. "From 'SSC' and 'RACK' to the '4Cs': Introducing a New Framework for Negotiating BDSM Participation." *Electronic Journal of Human Sexuality* 17 (August 2014). Williams and colleagues discuss how sexual negotiation works in the BDSM community, including "levels of consent" suitable for different stages of a sexual encounter.

CHAPTER 3: SCAFFOLDING GOOD SEX

Eaton, Anne W. "Taste in Bodies and Fat Oppression." In *Body Aesthetics*, ed. Sherri Irvin. Oxford University Press, 2016. Eaton argues that we are morally blameworthy for having sexual tastes that enforce oppressive norms, and suggests ways to alter our tastes to resist these norms.

Gahran, Amy. *Stepping Off the Relationship Escalator: Uncommon Love and Life.* Off the Escalator Enterprises, 2017. Gahran contends that our traditional understanding of romantic relationships is shaped by a narrow and limiting set of scripts and expectations.

Gavey, Nicola. *Just Sex? The Cultural Scaffolding of Rape*. Routledge, 2018. Gavey argues that mainstream heterosexual culture scaffolds rape through its scripts and social practices.

READINGS IN CONVERSATION 147

Langton, Rae. "Speech Acts and Unspeakable Acts." *Philosophy and Public Affairs* 22, no. 4 (Autumn 1993): 293–330. Langton argues that rape culture and pornography make it difficult or even impossible for women to refuse sex.

Manne, Kate. *Down Girl: The Logic of Misogyny.* Oxford University Press, 2017. Manne's influential work examines the pervasiveness of rape culture and misogynist norms in everyday life, showing how these forces shape our personal relationships and disempower women. She also provides a compelling analysis of incel culture.

Srinivasan, Amia. *The Right to Sex: Feminism in the Twenty-First Century.* Farrar, Straus and Giroux, 2022. Srinivasan's essays tackle complex questions about the "right to sex," our responsibility for sexual preferences, and the impact of rape culture.

CHAPTER 4: IMPERFECT AUTONOMY

Hay, Carol. *Think Like a Feminist: The Philosophy Behind the Revolution.* W. W. Norton, 2020. This is a lively, readable overview of feminism that contains an excellent discussion of the ways that gendered power relationships shape our lives.

Kukla, Quill R. "A Nonideal Theory of Sexual Consent." *Ethics* 131, no. 2 (2021). In this article, I develop my account of compromised autonomy and scaffolding one another's agency in more detail.

Lindemann, Hilde. *Holding and Letting Go: The Social Practice of Personal Identities.* Oxford University Press, 2014. Lindemann shows how people can help and support one another in being themselves; being oneself, she argues, is a scaffolded social achievement, not an individual one.

MacKinnon, Catharine. *Towards a Feminist Theory of the State.* Harvard University Press, 1989. A classic feminist treatise arguing that heterosexual sex is inextricable from misogyny and power relations.

Tarzia, Laura, Deirdre Fetherstonhaugh, and Michael Bauer. "Dementia, Sexuality, and Consent in Residential Aged Care Facilities." *Journal of Medical Ethics* 38,

148   READINGS IN CONVERSATION

no. 10 (October 2012): 609–13. This article explores consent and sexual agency among people with dementia living in care facilities.

Victor, Elizabeth, and Laura Guidry-Grimes. "Relational Autonomy in Action: Rethinking Dementia and Sexuality in Care Facilities." *Nursing Ethics* 26, no. 6 (September 2019): 1654–64. The authors explore how care facilities can support or undermine the sexual agency of residents with dementia.

CHAPTER 5: AMBIVALENCE AND AGENCY

Angel, Katherine. *Tomorrow the Sex Will Be Good Again: Women and Desire in the Age of Consent.* Verso, 2021. Angel argues that we don't always know what we want, especially when it comes to sex, and looks at how this ambivalence should shape our thinking about consent.

Dougherty, Tom. "Enthusiastic Consent to Sex." In *Palgrave Handbook of Sexual Ethics*, ed. David Boonin. Palgrave-Macmillan, 2021. Dougherty argues that enthusiasm is not a requirement for valid sexual consent.

CHAPTER 6: EXTRACTIVE SEX AND RAPE CULTURE

Cook, Bob. "Brock Turner's Dad Reveals How Rape Culture Seeds Get Planted in Youth Sports." *Forbes*, June 9, 2016. Cook discusses the case of Brock Turner, who raped an unconscious woman behind a dumpster after a college party, using it as a lens to explore how rape culture is perpetuated through youth sports, and how public reactions to such cases exemplify rape culture.

Kipnis, Laura. *Unwanted Advances: Sexual Paranoia Comes to Campus.* Verso, 2018. In this controversial book, Kipnis argues that the concept of rape culture on campuses has led to paranoia and a regressive sexual culture that disempowers women and fosters mistrust.

Manne, Kate. *Entitled: How Male Privilege Hurts Women.* Crown, 2020. Manne explores how men's feelings of entitlement to sex and rape culture are interconnected. She argues that society tends to exhibit *himpathy*, or sympathy for male perpetrators of sexual violence, often viewing them as having been unfairly treated.

READINGS IN CONVERSATION   149

CHAPTER 7: SEX WORK AND SEXUAL CONTRACTS

Flanigan, Jessica, and Lori Watson. *Debating Sex Work*. Oxford University Press, 2019. Two feminist philosophers debate whether sex work can be consensual and ethical, and whether and how it should be legal.

Lopez, Susan, Mariko Passion, and Saundra. "Who're You Calling a Whore? A Conversation with Three Sex Workers on Sexuality, Empowerment, and the Industry." In Friedman and Valenti. *Yes Means Yes! Visions of Female Sexual Power and a World Without Rape*. Seal Press, 2008. The title of the article is a summary of its contents!

CHAPTER 8: DOMINATION, SUBMISSION, AND POWER PLAY

Dougherty, Tom. "Sex, Lies, and Consent." *Ethics* 123, no. 4 (July 2013): 717–44. Dougherty argues that if a person consents to sex based on deception or misinformation, their consent is invalid.

Ebbe, Morten, and Juul Nielsen. "Safe, Sane, and Consensual—Consent and the Ethics of BDSM." *International Journal of Applied Philosophy* 24, no. 2 (2010): 265–88. This article examines when, whether, and how BDSM practices can be consensual and ethical.

Gordon, Mel. *Voluptuous Panic: The Erotic World of Weimar Berlin*. Feral House, 2008. This is an excellent history of the emergence of kink culture in early-twentieth-century Berlin.

Kali, Princess. *Enough to Make You Blush: Exploring Erotic Humiliation*. Erotication Publications, 2015. A celebrated professional domme and sex educator explores erotic humiliation, including when and how it can be practiced ethically, and what good negotiation and scaffolding for this kind of play look like.

Linden, Robin Ruth. *Against Sadomasochism: A Radical Feminist Analysis*. Frog in the Well, 1983. A classic collection of essays arguing from a second-wave feminist perspective that BDSM is essentially misogynist.

FOR FURTHER EXPLORATION

ON CONSENT AND SEXUAL NEGOTIATION

The *Yes Means Yes!* blog, a blog about sexual negotiation hosted by the editors of the *Yes Means Yes!* essay collection: https://yesmeansyesblog.wordpress.com/.

"Tea and Consent," a short and very influential 2015 video that compares sexual consent to consent to drinking tea: https://www.youtube.com/watch?v=oQbei5JGiT8&ab_channel=BlueSeatStudios.

"Have you seen that tea and consent video?," a blog post by sex educator Justin Hancock critiquing the "Tea and Consent" video, on his blog bishtraining.com.

"What Is Consent? How to Practically Apply Consent Before Sex," by Nona Willis Aronowitz in *Teen Vogue*, an excellent practical article on how to negotiate consent, written in 2021 and aimed at younger people. https://www.teenvogue.com/story/what-is-consent.

Heartbreak High, a 2022 Australian Netflix original series, set at a diverse Sydney high school, and exploring true-to-life scenarios involving teenage sex and sexual negotiation in a sophisticated way.

ON KINK, DOMINATION AND SUBMISSION, AND POWER PLAY

The Marquis de Sade's 1795 work *Philosophy in the Bedroom* is the original source on sadomasochism. The Marquis de Sade, from whose name we get the word

152 FOR FURTHER EXPLORATION

sadism, was imprisoned for his views on sexual freedom. Be warned that the book is very explicit.

Leopold von Sacher Masoch's *Venus in Furs*, written in 1870, is the original source of our word *masochism*. Like Sade's work, it helped form our imagination of what sadomasochistic sex and relationships look like. This book is also very explicit.

Romantic Agency: Loving Well in Modern Life (Polity, 2023), by philosopher Luke Brunning, is not technically on kink or power exchange, but it is an excellent and readable book about nonstandard romantic relationships.

The Gender and Sexual Therapy Center has an excellent blog that takes a kink-centered perspective on sex, gender identity, and sexual orientation: https://www.gstherapycenter.com/blog.

ON SEX WORK

If you want to find out more about sex work, please make sure that you are looking at resources created by sex workers rather than outsiders. There are many excellent blogs and online resources run by sex workers. A few of my favorites include:

https://titsandsass.com/, written by and for sex workers. No new content after 2020, but the archives contain great material.

tryst.link/blog, written by and for sex workers, with articles exploring all aspects of sex work and sex work advocacy, including the distinctive concerns of sex workers of color, trans sex workers, disabled sex workers, and more.

The Global Network of Sex Work Projects, https://www.nswp.org/, is an advocacy network with good online resources and information.

Jack Talks About Sex Work, https://jackviolet.com/, is a blog run by a trans sex worker.

FOR FURTHER EXPLORATION   153

ON SEXUAL ASSAULT

Some readers of this book may find parts of it hard to read if they have a history of experiencing sexual violence or abuse. Some readers may even come to realize through reading it that they have been sexually assaulted, violated, or mistreated. Here are some resources that may be of help to you if you are in this situation or just want to learn more about sexual assault.

The National Sexual Violence Resource center, at https://www.nsvrc.org/, is an excellent source of statistics, advocacy, and support for those in the United States.

The Sexual Assault Kit Initiative has a good list of hotlines, services for survivors, and other resources, at https://www.sakitta.org/survivors/.

INDEX

ableism, 70, 124, 141
abusive relationships, 82
academic settings, 65, 86–87
accessibility, of sexual agency, 52
accountability, 43, 83, 103–4
affirmative consent, 3, 6–7, 10, 13, 58, 76
aftercare, 125–27
agency, 125; *See also* sexual agency
   autonomy vs., 55
   bodily, for children, 36, 41–42
   holding one another in agency, 62–63
alcohol use, *See* intoxicated people
alternative sex communities, 5–6, 49; *See also specific types*
altruism, sexual, 111–12
ambivalence, 72–85, 105, 132–33
   and benefits of pushing limits, 78–79, 84, 85
   communication about, 83–85
   consent and, 75–78
   ethical dilemmas involving, 1–4, 72–74
   scaffolding agency with, 76, 79–83
   social punishment for, 82–83
   as universal experience, 74–75
anal sex, 48, 109
Angel, Katherine, 74–75, 77
Ansari, Aziz, 10
Antioch Policy, 13–14, 43, 74
appreciation, for good communication, 98
asexual people, 4, 32, 60
asking (speech act), 28
attraction, 46–47
autonomy, 53–71, 133; *See also* imperfect autonomy

aftercare to restore, 126
choosing to give up some, 121–23
contracts that limit, 110
defined, 55
and holding in agency, 62–63
ideal autonomous self, 54–55
minimal, 55–57
in sex work, 105
awareness team members, 127

bad sex; *See also* sexual violations
consenting to, 9, 10
extractive sex as, 93
lack of sexual negotiation and, 25
protecting against, 4–5
BDSM community, 117–18, 132; *See also* bondage; dominance–submission relationships; masochism; sadism
books on, 120–21
power play terminology from, 119–20
"risky" sex in, 124
role play and playing oneself for, 130
toxic social norms in, 128
Berlin, Germany, 121
bestiality, 141
bisexual people, 66, 94
Black men and boys, rape of, 90
bodily agency, for children, 36, 41–42
body language, 21, 24
body shaming, 46–47, 86, 87, 91–94, 99
bondage, 1–3, 28, 72–74, 130
bottom, *See* submissive (sub)
bottoming, definitions of, 144

156   INDEX

boundaries
  pushing, 78–79, 84, 85
  respecting, 42, 105, 106
brats, in kink community, 121
bystanders, harm to, 129–30

cam girls and camming, 100–101, 138
children
  bodily agency for, 36, 41–42
  parent-child sex for, 68–69
  pornography exposure for, 48–49
chill rooms, 127
cisgender people, centering, 6
coercion, 64, 77, 93, 96, 102, 106, 111
cognitive disabilities, people with, 71; *See
    also* dementia, people with
commodification, of human bodies, 101–2
commodity model of sex, 15–17, 88–89,
    101, 103, 109
communication; *See also* sexual
    communication
  about ambivalence, 83–85
  about communication, 24–25
  about joint activities, 21–22, 108–9
community scaffolding for sexual agency,
    18, 38–39, 44–46, 51, 68, 82
confidentiality, 43–44
confrontations, 35, 81
conscious decision-making, 55
consensual nonconsent, 119, 121–22, 126
consensual sex, 7–8, 54–56, 63, 66–67
consent, 133
  ableist view of, 141
  affirmative, 3, 6–7, 10, 13, 58, 76
  in ambivalent situations, 75–78
  contractual, 101
  defining, 137
  dominance of, 9–10
  enthusiastic, 32, 76–78, 105–8, 133
  FRIES model of, 77–78
  giving, 8–9, 27
  informed, 77
  legal context for, 19
  ongoing, 13–14
  for people with imperfect autonomy, 71
  and performance model of sex, 15–17
  in power play, 131–32

reversible, 77, 83, 104
sex education on, 4–5
sexual agency and, 2–3, 6–8
sexual communication and, 7, 29
sexual ethics focused on, 2–5, 14–15
in sexual vs. nonsexual situations, 106–9
for sex workers, 101, 102
social scripts on acts requiring, 48
specific, 77
traditional framework for, *See*
    traditional consent framework
unenthusiastic, 106–8
"Consent: It's as Simple as Tea" (video), 14
contracts and contracted activities, 101–5,
    109–10, 118
contractual consent, 101
criminalization, of sex work, 111
cucks, in kink community, 121
cultural scaffolding for sexual agency,
    50–51, 82; *See also* social scripts
Curry, Tommy, 90

darkrooms, 127
dealbreakers, disclosing, 131–32
dementia, people with, 1–3, 53, 56, 57, 59–62
Desclos, Anne, 121
dick pics, unsolicited, 33
direct force, autonomy limited by, 63–64
disabled people and disability community,
    41, 45, 51–52, 69–71, 111–12
disclose, duty to, 131–32
dom, *See* dominant
domestic spaces, safety in, 96–97
dominance–submission relationships, 138;
    See also BDSM community
  books on, 120–21
  motivations of participants, 121–22
  round-the-clock, 129
  sexual ethics in, 1–3, 115–16
  sexual negotiation in, 24
dominant (dom, domme, top), 119–24,
    128, 144
"Don't Say Gay" law, 41
Dougherty, Tom, 50, 131
drunken sex, *See* intoxicated people
dungeons, 127
duty to disclose, 131–32

INDEX 157

economic scaffolding, for agency, 40, 84, 109, 110, 113, 114
educational scaffolding for sexual agency, 18, 39–42; *See also* sex education
elder abuse, 61
enthusiastic consent model, 32, 76–78, 105–8, 133
erectile dysfunction, 44, 91
erotic conversation, 26, 138
exiting an activity
  agency and ability to leave, 40, 58, 61, 70, 79
  in ambivalent situations, 79–80, 83, 84
  for contracted activities, 103–5
  in power play, 124–25
  sexual negotiation of, 33–36
exploitation, 30, 55, 102, 110, 112, 117, 118
extractive sex, 88–90, 93, 97–99

families, power differentials in, 68–69
fat people, 46, 92
fear-based sexual ethics, 133
feminism, 4, 67, 116, 141
feminist pornography, 49
financial domination, 129
forced service, 120, 122
force of speech, 27–29
freedom, 19, 77, 90–91, 133
FRIES model of consent, 77–78
fully autonomous self, 116, 140
furries, 130

Gahran, Amy, 49
Garcia, Manon, 11, 48, 68, 118
gender relations, predator–prey framing of, 94–97, 142
gender fluid people, 131
gender swapping role-play, 130–31
Generation Z, 6
generosity, sexual, 31–33, 105, 112
gift-giving, 31–33, 139
gift offers, 31–33, 105
Goodyear, Trevor, 57
Gow, Joe, 100, 102, 106, 112–14
gratitude, for sexual invitation, 30–31
green, yellow, red system, 34
group sex, 6, 100, 113

hairy men, 92
heterosexual sex, 5, 6
  asymmetries in, 11–12, 88
  extractive, 88–90
  power differentials in, 65–67, 128
  power play and, 117–18, 128
  sexual negotiation in, 25–26
  social scripts for, 47–48, 50
holding in agency, 62–63
holding in personhood, 62
homeless people, 40
homophobia, 45, 94
homosexuality, medicalization of, 44
hookup sex, 6, 65, 131–32
humiliation, 120, 122, 126, 129–30

Icarus, 68, 84, 98, 124, 128, 133
ideal autonomous self, 54–55
identity, experimenting with, 130–31
imperfect autonomy, 140
  ability to give consent with, 71
  due to ambivalence, 75–76
  ethical dilemmas involving, 53–54
  and good sex, 54–55
  internal vs. external reasons for, 54, 57
  for intoxicated people, 57–59
  for people with dementia, 59–62
  in power differentials, 63–71
incels, 89
independence, 51–52, 55
infants, sexually pleasuring, 141
informed consent, 77
initiation of sex
  consent at, 9, 13–14, 79–80
  with imperfect autonomy, 57–61
  involving power play, 123–24
  sexual negotiation for, 28–33
institutional scaffolding for sexual agency, 40, 43–44
  in ambivalent situations, 84
  good vs. bad, 18, 132
  with imperfect autonomy, 68
  for sex workers, 109
internalized shame, 46
interpersonal scaffolding for sexual agency, 18, 39, 51, 55, 84, 109
intersex people, 41, 46

158 INDEX

intimate work, nonsexual, 104–5
intoxicated people, 1–4, 53–59, 71
inviting (speech act), 27, 29–31

James, E. L., 121
Jaworska, Agnieszka, 56
joint activities (nonsexual)
 ambivalence about, 72–74
 communicating about, 21–22, 108–9
 consent for, 8, 76–77, 106–9
 contracted, 104–5
 exiting, 80–81, 103–5, 125
 giving up power/control in, 123

kink community, 5–6
 aftercare in, 125
 body diversity in, 94
 cultural and community scaffolding
  in, 82
 ethical dilemmas involving, 128–30
 FRIES model of consent in, 77–78
 historical context for culture of, 120–21
 power play in, 116–19
 risk aware consensual sex in, 124
 sexual negotiation in, 23–25, 128–29
 social scripts in, 51
 terminology for power play from, 119–20

leave, ability to, 40, 58, 61, 70, 79
legal scaffolding for sexual agency, 18, 39,
  43–44, 51, 109
Lief, 84, 98, 128
Lindemann, Hilde, 62
long-term care homes, 60–61
long-term relationships, 31–33, 62–63,
  65–66, 101, 129, 132; *See also*
  marriage
love, as excuse for violation, 70–71

Manne, Kate, 66
marijuana use, *See* intoxicated people
marriage, 15, 49, 54, 103, 128
masochism, 120, 122
material scaffolding for sexual agency, 39,
  50
 in ambivalent situations, 81, 84
 good vs. bad, 18, 132

in kink communities, 121, 127
for sex workers, 109
McDowell, Josh, 15–16
McMahan, Jeff, 70–71
medical settings, 44, 56, 57, 64–65, 104
men
 on alcohol and good sex, 57–58
 autonomy under patriarchy for, 65–67
 body shaming of, 86, 87, 91–93, 99
 celebrating beauty of, 93–94
 erectile dysfunction for, 44, 91
 extractive sex for, 88–90
 gratitude for sexual invitation from, 31
 performance model of sex for, 15
 power play for, 117–18
 in predator–prey framing, 94–95
 rape culture and agency of, 91–95, 98–99
 roles of, in BDSM, 128
 scripts on sexual pleasure for, 70–71
 sex as asymmetric encounter between
  women and, 11–12, 88
 sexual needs/vulnerabilities of, 12, 75
 sexual negotiation by, 25
 as sexual objects, 90, 142
 social scripts in vanilla sex for, 47–48
 strip clubs for, 92
 violence in public spaces against, 95–96
Millar, Thomas MacAulay, 15, 88
minimal autonomy, 55–57
misogyny, 48, 67, 71, 129
Momoa, Jason, 108
monogamy, 5, 6, 16, 49, 89, 101; *See also*
  vanilla sex

National Sexual Violence Resource Center,
  142–43
negative freedom, 19
nonbinary people, 75, 99
nonconsensual sex, 4, 68–71, 106; *See also*
  rape
nonsexual joint activities, *See* joint
  activities (nonsexual)
nonverbal communication, 22–23

obligations, 31–32, 103–4
offering (speech act), 31–33
older people, 45, 59–61

INDEX 159

ongoing consent, 13–14
OnlyFans, 100
oral sex, 58–59, 120
ordering (speech act), 27, 28

pain, 120, 122, 123
parent-child sex, 68–69
patriarchy, 65–67, 128
penis, body shaming focused on, 91–92
performance model of sex, 15–17
permission, 12–13, 108
personhood, holding in, 62
physical environment, scaffolding for sexual
        agency in, 18, 40, 60, 127; *See also*
        material scaffolding for sexual agency
physical harm, 115–16, 119, 120
play, in kink community
    defined, 119
    role-play vs. playing oneself, 130–31
play spaces, 127
policies, scaffolding for sexual agency by,
        40, 43, 65
pornography, 48–49, 100, 106, 111–14, 118
positive freedom, 19
power differentials; *See also* power play
    in BDSM, 128
    imperfect autonomy in, 52, 54, 63–71
    minimal autonomy in, 56
    in rape culture, 86–87
    during sexual negotiation, 128–29
    and traditional consent framework, 116
power exchange, 143
power play, 115–32
    and aftercare, 125–27
    ethical dilemmas involving, 115–16,
        118–19, 127–32
    history of, 120–21
    in kink and BDSM communities,
        117–18
    motivations of participants in, 121–23
    privacy and consent in, 131–32
    role play and playing oneself in, 130–31
    sexual negotiation in, 118, 123–25, 130
    terminology associated with, 119–20
    traditional consent framework for, 116
    universal appeal of, 116–18
predator–prey framing of gender, 94–97, 142

PrEP, 44
privacy, 40, 52, 60, 105, 127, 131–32
promises, 28, 83
promises, sexual, 138–39
public spaces, safety in, 95–97
"puppies," in kink community, 121

queer people and queer community, 5–6
    masculine beauty in, 93–94
    in prewar Berlin, 121
    rape and sexual assault risk for, 90
    rape culture and agency of, 99
    scaffolding for agency for, 37–39, 45
    sex education that shames, 41
    social scripts for, 48, 82–83

racism, 71, 90, 130
rape
    autonomy and, 66, 67, 69–71
    and knowledge of permission, 108
    labeling sex work as, 105–6
    prevalence of, 99
    prevalence vs. fear of, 95–96
    in rape culture, 88, 95–96
    sex education focusing on, 4, 5, 41–42
    types of, 90
rape culture, 86–99
    body shaming in, 91–94
    defined, 88
    dismantling, 99
    ethical issues perpetuated by, 86–87
    extractive sex in, 88–90
    predator–prey framing in, 94–97, 142
    refusal of sex in, 97–99
    sexual agency in, 90–91
    sexual negotiation in, 97–99
Rayhons, Donna Lou, 53
Rayhons, Henry, 53, 61
reciprocation, 32–33
refusing (speech act), 27
refusing sex
    autonomy and, 66, 69
    in healthy culture of sexuality, 98
    in predator–prey model, 97–98
    in rape culture, 90–91, 97–99
    in traditional model of consent, 5–7,
        12–13, 76, 133

160 INDEX

relationship escalator, 49–50
requesting (speech act), 8–9, 27–30
responsibility, to communicate
  ambivalence, 84
restraint, 12–13
reversible consent, 77, 83, 104
risk-aware consensual sex, 124
role play, 26, 127, 130–31
romantic relationships
  extractive sex in, 89–90
  long-term, 31–33, 62–63, 65–66, 101,
    129, 132
  marriage, 15, 49, 54, 103, 128
  social scripts for, 49–50

Sacher-Masoch, Leopold von, 120
Sade, Marquis de, 120
sadism, 120, 123
safer sex tools, 127
safety, 95–97, 102, 111, 127
safe words, 34–36, 50, 80, 81, 125
Savage, Dan, 126
  campsite rule, 126–27
scaffolding for sexual agency, 37–52, 132;
    See also specific types, e.g.: material
    scaffolding for sexual agency
  in ambivalent situations, 76, 79–83
  in BDSM community, 118
  body shaming, attraction, and, 46–47
  ethical dilemma involving, 37–39
  with imperfect autonomy, 55, 57–61
  in power play, 126–27
  safe words in, 34
  sexual negotiation in, 98
  in sex work, 101, 109–11, 113–14
  variations in, 17–19
scene (in a kink or BDSM context), 24,
    81–82, 118–19, 126, 128–32
  defined, 119
  how to exit, 36
  negotiation of, 36, 124, 129
  role-playing in, 130–31
  spaces for, 127
second-wave feminism, 141
secrecy, 44–45, 60–61, 110, 132
self-determination, 132
  and ability to exit activity, 33

in ambivalent situations, 82, 85
full, 18
independence, agency, and, 51–52
in sexual vs. regular consent, 106–7
in sex work, 101
self-esteem, men's, 92–93
Serano, Julia, 95
sex education, 4–6, 35–36, 40–43, 52
sex toys, 52, 115, 120, 123
sex trafficking, 102
sexual agency; *See also* scaffolding for
    sexual agency
  accessibility of, 52
  ambiguity about, 5, 19–20
  and consent, 2–3, 6–8
  defined, 2
  determining, 3–4
  ethical dilemmas involving, 1–4
  expanding, 34, 78–79, 84, 85
  frameworks for, 133
  good sex to enhance, 5–6
  heterosexual sex as paradigm for, 6
  independence, self-determination, and,
    51–52
  and positive vs. negative freedom, 19
  power play as expression of, 117
  protecting partner's, 84–85
  in rape culture, 90–91
  for sex workers, 101–3, 112–14
sexual altruism, 111–12
sexual assault, 66, 90, 96
sexual communication; *See also* sexual
    negotiation
  beyond consent, 14–15
  flattening of, 10–11
  for good sex, 7, 10–11, 14, 22–23
  imperfect autonomy and, 58–62
  in rape culture, 97–98
sexual contracts, 102–5, 109–10
sexual ethics
  and ambivalence, 72–74
  of attraction, 46–47
  communication about, 24–25
  communication in, 26
  consent as focus of, 2–8, 14–15
  consenting to sex that violates, 9–10
  fear-based, 133

INDEX 161

of imperfect autonomy, 53–56
of play without easy exit conditions, 125
of power play, 115–16, 118–19, 127–30
in rape culture, 86–87
in relationships, aside from consent, 140–41
and sexual agency, 1–4, 8, 37–39
of sex work, 100–102, 109, 112, 114
sexual exploration, 63, 82–83
sexual generosity, 31–33, 105, 112
sexual harassment, 30–31, 86–87
sexual intimacy, dementia and desire for, 59–61
sexual misconduct, 10
sexual negotiation, 6, 132, 138
  about exiting activity, 33–36, 81–82
  on aftercare, 125–26
  complexity of, 36
  defined, 23
  difficulties with, 26–27
  equality in, 128–29
  in extractive sex, 88
  in healthy culture of sexuality, 98, 99
  to initiate sex, 29–33
  in kink community, 23–25
  minimal autonomy for, 58–59
  under patriarchy, 68
  in power play, 118, 119, 123–25, 130
  in rape culture, 97–99
  role-play and, 130–31
  sex education on, 41
  in sex work, 102–4
  social scripts and, 48
  speech acts in, 27–29
  in traditional model of consent, 11–13
  between vanilla sex partners, 25–26
sexual promises, 138–39
sexual violations, 4, 67; *See also* rape
  love as excuse for, 70–71
  reporting, 43–44
  sexual assault, 66, 90, 96
  sexual harassment, 30–31, 86–87
  sexual misconduct, 10
sex work, 6, 100–114
  and enthusiastic consent, 105–8
  ethical dilemma involving, 100–102, 109, 112, 114

and exiting contracted activities, 103–5
forms of, 100
motivations of sex workers, 111–13
objections to, 101–2
scaffolding for sexual agency in, 109–11
sexual agency for sex workers, 101–3, 112–14
and sexual consent vs. regular consent, 108–9
shame, 41, 46–47, 82–83, 110, 113
Shane, Charlotte, 105–6
Singer, Peter, 70–71
"sleep," power play involving, 123–24
social isolation, 45, 96
social norms, 32–33, 97, 128
social scaffolding for sexual agency, 39–40
  in ambivalent situations, 84
  good vs. bad, 18, 19, 132
  with imperfect autonomy, 55, 60, 65–68
  in kink communities, 121
  for sex workers, 102, 109, 110
social scripts, 47–51, 82–83, 99
social support, for holding in agency, 62–63
specific consent, 77
speech acts, 27–29
speech act theory, 27, 138
Srinivasan, Amia, 46, 93
stigmatization, 45, 47, 69, 111, 113
stoned sex, *See* intoxicated people
strippers, 92, 138
Stubblefield, Anna, 69–71
submission, desire for, 116, 117; *See also* BDSM community; dominance–submission relationships
submissive (sub, bottom), 119–22, 126, 128, 144
sugaring, defined, 100
suggesting (speech act), 27

"take back the night" marches, 96
Tame, Grace, 43
teens
  imperfect autonomy for, 54, 71
  pornography exposure for, 48–49
  scaffolding for sexual agency of, 44–45
  sex education for, 35–36, 41–42

162 INDEX

Tits and Sass blog, 105
top, *See* dominant (dom, domme)
topping, definitions of, 144
touching, 42, 60, 127
traditional consent framework
in ambivalent situations, 77, 79–80
limitations of, 9–14
for power play, 116
refusing sex in, 5–7, 12–13, 76, 133
requesting sex in, 28
on sexual communication/negotiation,
22, 23
trans people
in alternative sex communities, 5–6
body shaming of, 92
rape and sexual assault risk for, 90
scaffolding agency for, 37–39, 41, 45,
46
shame over detransitioning for, 82
Tuerkheimer, Deborah, 55

ugly women, 92
unenthusiastic consent, 106–8
United States Military, 57
University of Wisconsin–La Crosse, 100,
113–14
US Department of Justice, 90, 143

vanilla sex, 5
elements of BDSM or power play in,
120
financial domination and, 129
negotiating aftercare in, 126
power differentials in, 128
power play in, 117

sexual negotiation in, 25–26
social scripts for, 47–48
Viagra, 44
virginity, 15–16

warning (speech act), 27
white women, rape perpetrated by, 90
will of sex partner, respecting, 108–9
Wilson, Carmen, 100, 102, 106, 112–14
Winter Fire, 23–24
Wit (Edson), 140
women
autonomy under patriarchy for, 65–68
desirability of bodies of, 86–87, 89,
91–93, 142
direct request to stop sex from, 35
extractive sex for, 88–90
gratitude of, for sexual invitation, 31
imperfect autonomy for, 54, 65–68
performance model of sex for, 15
power play in vanilla sex for, 117–18
in predator–prey framing, 94–95
rape culture and agency of, 90–91,
95–96, 98–99
refusal of sex by, 143
roles of, in BDSM, 128
sex as asymmetric encounter between
men and, 11–12, 88
sexual agency for, 5, 11–12
as sexual aggressors, 90, 142
sexual ambivalence for, 75
sexual negotiation by, 25
social scripts in vanilla sex for, 47–48
strip clubs for, 92
violence against, 95–97

Norton Shorts

BRILLIANCE WITH BREVITY

W. W. Norton & Company has been independent since 1923, when William Warder Norton and Mary (Polly) D. Herter Norton first published lectures delivered at the People's Institute, the adult education division of New York City's Cooper Union. In the 1950s, Polly Norton transferred control of the company to its employees.

One hundred years after its founding, W. W. Norton & Company inaugurates a new century of visionary independent publishing with Norton Shorts. Written by leading-edge scholars, these eye-opening books deliver bold thinking and fresh perspectives in under two hundred pages.

Available Fall 2025

Imagination: A Manifesto by Ruha Benjamin

What's Real About Race?: Untangling Science, Genetics, and Society by Rina Bliss

Offshore: Stealth Wealth and the New Colonialism by Brooke Harrington

Sex Beyond "Yes": Pleasure and Agency for Everyone by Quill R Kukla

Fewer Rules, Better People: The Case for Discretion by Barry Lam

Explorers: A New History by Matthew Lockwood

Wild Girls: How the Outdoors Shaped the Women Who Challenged a Nation by Tiya Miles

The Trafficker Next Door: How Household Employers Exploit Domestic Workers by Rhacel Salazar Parreñas

The Moral Circle: Who Matters, What Matters, and Why by Jeff Sebo

Against Technoableism: Rethinking Who Needs Improvement by Ashley Shew

Fear Less: Poetry in Perilous Times by Tracy K. Smith

Literary Theory for Robots: How Computers Learned to Write by Dennis Yi Tenen

Forthcoming

Mehrsa Baradaran on the racial wealth gap

Merlin Chowkwanyun on the social determinants of health

Daniel Aldana Cohen on eco-apartheid

Jim Downs on cultural healing

Reginald K. Ellis on Black education versus Black freedom

Nicole Eustace on settler colonialism

Agustín Fuentes on human nature

Justene Hill Edwards on the history of inequality in America

Destin Jenkins on a short history of debt

Kelly Lytle Hernández on the immigration regime in America

Natalia Molina on the myth of assimilation

Tony Perry on water in African American culture and history

Beth Piatote on living with history

Ashanté Reese on the transformative possibilities of food

Daniel Steinmetz-Jenkins on religion and populism

Onaje X. O. Woodbine on transcendence in sports